THE ART OF CANTILLATION
Volume 2

Ta-amei Hamikra • טַעֲמֵי הַמִּקְרָא

A STEP-BY-STEP GUIDE TO
CHANTING HAFTARAH AND *M'GILLOT*

Marshall Portnoy

Josée Wolff

Sally Neff, Project Editor

UAHC Department of Synagogue Music

Acknowledgments

We thank the following people:

Sally Neff, for her outstanding work as an intern; Bryna Fischer and Helene Denenberg, for their thoughtful editing and proof reading; Ken Gesser, of the UAHC Press, for his patience; Itzhack Shelomi, for making the text visually appealing; Uptime Studios, for their recording work; Andy Cohen, for his help with finale; Dr. Jane Portnoy for her inspiration and support; and all of our colleagues and students who gave us invaluable feedback along the way.

Marshall Portnoy

Josée Wolff

Contents

Introduction

> We are coming home to Torah because it is the very essence of our being and because we see as our first duty and greatest joy the teaching of those sacred texts that bind us to a shared faith and a shared way of life.
>
> —Rabbi Eric H. Yoffie, President, UAHC

The chanting of sacred text has always been the most basic and significant way of transmitting our tradition. Knowledge of the trope or cantillation system is crucial not only to the understanding of our sacred text but also to its correct pronunciation and phrasing. It is our goal to train more and more members of our communities to become capable Torah and haftarah readers and trope teachers. We hope that in the future, every UAHC congregation will have at least one Torah and haftarah reader among its members.

To reach this goal, the UAHC Department of Synagogue Music has developed two textbooks: *The Art of Torah Cantillation:* טַעֲמֵי הַמִּקְרָא and *The Art of Cantillation, Volume 2*. These materials are intended for use by any student who possesses a basic level of Hebrew-reading fluency and is interested in learning how to chant. The volumes may also be utilized by teachers who wish to fine-tune their cantillation skills.

The trope taught in this curriculum and presented on the accompanying CD is the version taught at Hebrew Union College–Jewish Institute of Religion, School of Sacred Music in New York. It is based on the musical notations of A. W. Binder and Cantor Lawrence Avery. This is the version that is most commonly used in Reform congregations throughout North America.

All of the examples and exercises in the book are recorded on the accompanying CD. The numeral printed next to each exercise corresponds to the track or ID number on the CD. Numbered musical notes next to some trope patterns are cross-references to the musical notation of the haftarah cantillation in Appendix D.

Ben Bag Bag used to say about Torah: "Turn it, and turn it, for everything is in it" (*Pirkei Avot* 5:22). May טַעֲמֵי הַמִּקְרָא provide you with yet another avenue to find more meaning in our sacred texts so that you may be inspired to continue on the lifelong journey of תַּלְמוּד תּוֹרָה, the study of Torah.

Cantor Josée Wolff
UAHC Department of Synagogue Music
New York, Tamuz 5761/ July 2001

LESSON 1

Chanting a Phrase From Haftarah

The *Etnachta* Clause • מַעֲרֶכֶת אֶתְנַחְתָּא

A הַפְטָרָה (haftarah) is a reading from the second section of the תנ"ך (*Tanach*), called נְבִיאִים (*N'vi-im*) or Prophets. This selection from Prophets concludes the biblical readings on Shabbat and holidays and is usually chanted immediately following the Torah reading. Often, the haftarah text has a direct thematic relationship to the Torah portion. Just as the reading of each section from a Torah portion is sandwiched by *b'rachot* (blessings) before and after, so too the haftarah reading is preceded and followed by special *b'rachot*. The *b'rachah* (blessing) before the reading is chanted according to the haftarah cantillation you will be learning in this book. The *b'rachot* after the haftarah are sung to melodies that are not specifically related to cantillation.[1]

What is cantillation? Biblical cantillation is the system that determines the way in which we read and chant from the *Tanach*. Cantillation helps the reader interpret the biblical text the way it was intended. It accomplishes this in the following ways:

- Cantillation functions as punctuation. It groups words together correctly and helps the reader pause at the appropriate places within each verse of the text. Without the use of punctuation, the intended meaning of a text may be unclear, as in the following example:

  Private Beach No Swimming Allowed

  You might interpret it as:

  Private beach. No swimming allowed.

  But with different punctuation, you might read it as follows:

  Private Beach? No! Swimming allowed.

- Cantillation also helps the reader accent the correct syllable. How do you know whether to say **PRO**-ject or pro-**JECT**, בָּנוּ (*ba-NU:* they built) or בָּנוּ (*BA-nu:* us)? The cantillation symbols indicate the correct placement of the accent and thus ensure that

---

[1] Appendix C contains a list of haftarot used in traditional and Reform congregations. You will find the musical notation for the *b'rachot* in Appendix D.

the reader does not inadvertently change the meaning of the text by accenting the wrong syllable.

- Furthermore, the cantillation you are about to learn adds a pleasant melody to the words. This melody is a nice "extra" because it helps us remember the text (Did you ever try to *say* "The Star-Spangled Banner"?) and makes the text much more enjoyable to hear.

The biblical cantillation system consists of twenty-eight symbols that tell you exactly how to punctuate the verses, on which syllable to stress each word, and how to chant each word or phrase. The Hebrew term for the cantillation symbols is טַעֲמֵי הַמִּקְרָא (*ta-amei hamikra*). The Hebrew word טַעַם means "taste" as well as "sense." The cantillation symbols literally help us make sense out of the text and give it its special "flavor." The symbols generally appear as part of a set pattern or phrase. We use the word "clause"—in Hebrew, מַעֲרֶכֶת (*ma-arechet*)—for each of those phrases.

The cantillation symbols you'll learn for haftarah look identical to the ones used in Torah and have the same names and the same functions. Those students that have already learned Torah cantillation will notice, however, that the melodies used for haftarah are quite different. It is this difference in melody that infuses each part of *Tanach* with its own distinctive *ta-am* or musical flavor.

Here's how the system works. Each sign or symbol stands for a musical pattern. For example, the symbol ֔ written beneath a word stands for the following musical pattern:

This symbol is called מֵרְכָא (*mercha*), and it is chanted like this:

מֵרְכָא

Now let's apply מֵרְכָא to a word. Just for fun, let's put it beneath the English word "hello."

Can you chant the word? You should have chanted it like this:　　　　hello

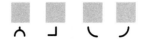

מֶרְכָא is one of the symbols used in cantillation. The symbols may look like curves, little lines, dots, or squiggles. Some appear beneath a word, some above it. In cantillation we call such a symbol a "trope." Some people use the word "trope" for the entire study of cantillation. You just learned the trope מֶרְכָא. Now try using it with a familiar Hebrew word. The word אֲשֶׁר means "which." How would you chant it with מֶרְכָא?

אֲשֶׁר

You may have noticed that not only is the trope notated beneath the word, but it appears beneath the very part of the word that should be stressed:

helLO, אֲשֶׁר.

Therefore, one of the most important things cantillation does is indicate which syllable in a word should be stressed. The placement of the trope tells us to say not **HEL**-lo but hel-**LO**, not *A-sher* but *a-SHER*.

> **With a few exceptions, the trope is notated above or below the first letter of the stressed syllable. If there is a vowel below the letter, the trope is notated to the left of the vowel.**

Here are a few examples with the trope מֶרְכָא. To practice, read the Hebrew word first, then sing the trope, and finally chant the words.

מֶרְכָא

יָמְין

הָיָה

עֵינֵי

רָקַע

You probably have noticed that the words you just practiced fit the melody of מֶרְכָא exactly because, like the word *mercha*, they all have two syllables. When the actual word in a haftarah text has more (or fewer) syllables than the name of the trope, you have to be flexible with the melody.

Every trope melody has two parts to it, a preparatory note or notes and the main melodic motif that falls on the accented syllable. Listen again to מֵרְכָא in example 2. The preparatory note can be heard on the syllable מֵרְ, and the main melodic motif then falls on the accented syllable כָא. When a word has more than one syllable before the accented syllable, as in וַחֲמִשִּׁים, repeat the preparatory note until you reach the accented syllable and then sing the main melodic motif. For the following words, sing the first note of מֵרְכָא as many times as necessary until you reach the accented syllable (where the trope is):

וְרָצָה

וַחֲמִשִּׁים

וְיִשָּׁבַע

What happens when a word is accented on the first syllable, or when there is only one syllable? In this case, the preparatory note is not chanted; only the main melodic motif is chanted. Try these examples:

קוּם

לֶחֶם

מֶלֶךְ

When a word has additional syllables after the accented syllable, divide the melody. The preparatory note is repeated until the accented syllable, followed by the rest of the melody. Try these examples:

בָּרֶגַע

וַיֹּאמֶר

קְרָאתִיךָ

מֶרְכָא is only one of the four tropes that form the *etnachta* clause. It often appears together with a trope that looks like its mirror image:

This trope is called טִפְחָא *(tipcha)* and sounds like this:

טִפְחָא

Together the two tropes sound like this:

מֶרְכָא טִפְחָא

Now chant this combination in a few different ways. For each example, first chant the tropes and then listen to the CD.

טִפְחָא
מֶרְכָא
טִפְחָא מֶרְכָא
מֶרְכָא טִפְחָא

Chant the following words with טִפְחָא:

טִפְחָא
יְרֵא
לִבּוֹ
בְּדִבְרֵיהֶם
לִפְקֹחַ

In the following examples, first chant the tropes by their names and then chant the actual words. Listen to the recording to hear each phrase chanted correctly.

 6

הָיָה יָרֵא

וְרָצָה בְדִבְרֵיהֶם

וְאַמֵּיץ לִבּוֹ

קְרָאתִיךָ בְצֶדֶק

If a טִפְחָא falls on a one-syllable word, sing only the second note of the טִפְחָא melody (which is the main melodic motif). Try to chant the following examples:

7

עָם

לִבְרִית עָם

אִישׁ

וַחֲמִשִּׁים אִישׁ

Now you're ready to learn the trope that gives this clause its name: אֶתְנַחְתָּא (etnachta). אֶתְנַחְתָּא looks just like a wishbone and is notated beneath a word:

It sounds like this:

אֶתְנַחְתָּא **8**

Now try a few words using אֶתְנַחְתָּא:

אֶתְנַחְתָּא

בֶּאֱמֶת

בַּגִּבּוֹרִים

מִיָּמִים

הִנֵּה־בָאוּ

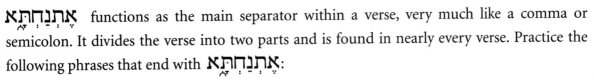

אֶתְנַחְתָּא functions as the main separator within a verse, very much like a comma or semicolon. It divides the verse into two parts and is found in nearly every verse. Practice the following phrases that end with אֶתְנַחְתָּא:

מֵרְכָא טִפְחָא אֶתְנַחְתָּא

וְאַמִּיץ לִבּוֹ בַּגִּבּוֹרִים

הֵילְכוּ שְׁנַיִם יַחְדָּו

טִפְחָא אֶתְנַחְתָּא

וַיִּגַּע עַל־פִּי

וַיְהִי מִיָּמִים

So far, you've learned אֶתְנַחְתָּא clauses of two and three words in the following two patterns:

מֵרְכָא טִפְחָא אֶתְנַחְתָּא

טִפְחָא אֶתְנַחְתָּא

One additional trope completes the _etnachta_ clause. This trope is called מֻנַּח (_munach_). It appears beneath a word and looks like a right angle:

מֻנַּח is a "servant" trope because it always appears in combination with אֶתְנַחְתָּא and other tropes, but never on its own. מֻנַּח functions not as a separator but as a connector of words and phrases. When it appears before אֶתְנַחְתָּא, it sounds like this:

מֻנַּח אֶתְנַחְתָּא

Here are some examples:

מִנָּח אֶתְנַחְתָּא 🔟

הַנֶּאֱמָרִים בֶּאֱמֶת

וְאַחְזֵק בְּיָדֶךָ

מִקְצֵה הָאָרֶץ

When מִנָּח follows טִפְחָא, it begins on the same note on which טִפְחָא ends:

טִפְחָא ◄ מִנָּח אֶתְנַחְתָּא 1️⃣1️⃣

בְּדִבְרֵיהֶם הַנֶּאֱמָרִים בֶּאֱמֶת

אֶל־הַיַּבָּשָׁה וְלֹא יָכְלוּ

אֶל־נִינְוֵה הָעִיר הַגְּדוֹלָה

Here are the most common variations of the *etnachta* clause:

מֶרְכָא טִפְחָא מִנָּח אֶתְנַחְתָּא ♪1 1️⃣2️⃣

טִפְחָא מִנָּח אֶתְנַחְתָּא ♪2

מִנָּח אֶתְנַחְתָּא

מֶרְכָא טִפְחָא אֶתְנַחְתָּא ♪3

טִפְחָא אֶתְנַחְתָּא ♪4

You are now ready to practice some examples from *N'vi-im*. It might be helpful to follow these three steps:

1. Read the Hebrew words.
2. Chant the tropes, using their names.
3. Chant the text.

The blessing before the reading of the haftarah is chanted according to the haftarah cantillation. It is helpful to refer to this blessing to aid in your understanding of the tropes. One of the phrases from the blessing is an *etnachta* clause:

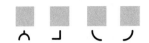

וְרָצָה בְדִבְרֵיהֶם הַנֶּאֱמָרִים בֶּאֱמֶת

...and has been pleased with their words of truth... (blessing before the reading of the haftarah)

רֹקַע הָאָרֶץ וְצֶאֱצָאֶיהָ

...He who spread forth the earth and that which came out of it... (Isaiah 42:5)[2]

קְרָאתִיךָ בְצֶדֶק וְאַחְזֵק בְּיָדֶךָ

I have called you in righteousness and will hold your hand. (Isaiah 42:6)

לִפְקֹחַ עֵינַיִם עִוְרוֹת

...To open the blind eyes... (Isaiah 42:7)

הָרִאשֹׁנוֹת הִנֵּה־בָאוּ

Behold, the former things have come to pass. (Isaiah 42:9)

תְּהִלָּתוֹ מִקְצֵה הָאָרֶץ

[Sing] His praise from the end of the earth. (Isaiah 42:10)

---

2 If you want to refer to a particular chapter and verse in *Tanach*, it is customary to insert a colon between the chapter and the verse. For example, the first verse of the Book of Isaiah is notated as Isaiah 1:1. If more than one chapter or verse is cited, a dash is used. Thus Isaiah 42:5–10 means the Book of Isaiah, chapter 42, verses 5 through 10, and 2 Samuel 6:1–7:17 means the Second Book of Samuel, chapter 6, verse 1, through chapter 7, verse 17.

Ending a Verse of Haftarah

The *Sof-Pasuk* Clause • מַעֲרֶכֶת סוֹף־פָּסוּק

As noted earlier, the most important purpose of cantillation is to indicate where to pause when reading the words of the *Tanach* so that the intended meaning of the text is clear. The most significant pause in any verse, or פָּסוּק (*pasuk*),[3] of *Tanach* is, of course, its concluding word, just as the most significant pause in any sentence is its final word. In English, that pause is denoted by a period that follows the final word. In the *Tanach*, that pause is denoted by an accent mark called a מֶתֶג (*meteg*)—a vertical line that appears below the final word—followed by two thick, vertical, diamondlike dots that look just like a colon:

The cantillation of the final word of a verse is called סוֹף־פָּסוּק (*sof-pasuk*), literally, "end of verse." Here are some examples of *sof-pasuk*:

סוֹף־פָּסוּק: **14**

יִתְגַּבָּר:

וְיַאְדִּיר:

וְצָדֵק:

אַף־מְרוֹמֵם:

כֵּאלֹהֵינוּ:

Only when both the colon and the accent mark are present do we encounter the concluding word of a פָּסוּק.

---

[3] Two words that we frequently use when discussing *Tanach* are the Hebrew word for "chapter," which is פֶּרֶק (*perek*), and the Hebrew word for "verse," which is פָּסוּק (*pasuk*). For a more complete glossary of terms, see Appendix H.

A vertical line notated under a word and *not* followed by a colon is simply a מֶתֶג, an accent mark indicating (secondary) accents in the word. It has no melody associated with it. If you see a vertical line under a word and you are not sure what it is, always look for a colon. If a colon follows the word, you need to chant סוֹף־פָּסוּק:. If there is no colon, you don't have to worry about melody—just make sure you stress the indicated syllable.

The first two tropes you learned, מֵרְכָא and טִפְחָא, may also appear as part of the *sof-pasuk* clause. However, in the *sof-pasuk* clause they have a different melody than they do in the *etnachta* clause. This represents a significant change from Torah cantillation, in which טִפְחָא and מֵרְכָא sound the same in both clauses.

When טִפְחָא and מֵרְכָא appear as part of a *sof-pasuk* clause,

they have a different melody.

Whenever you prepare a haftarah portion, always look ahead to see whether טִפְחָא or מֵרְכָא are part of a *sof-pasuk* or an *etnachta* clause. Then you will know how to chant the tropes. Here are some examples of *sof-pasuk* clauses:

טִפְחָא סוֹף־פָּסוּק:

עַל־אֹיְבָיו יִתְגַּבָּר:

מַשְׁפִּיל אַף־מְרוֹמֵם:

מֵרְכָא טִפְחָא סוֹף־פָּסוּק:

וּבִנְבִיאֵי הָאֱמֶת וָצֶדֶק:

יַגְדִּיל תּוֹרָה וְיַאְדִּיר:

מֵרְכָא טִפְחָא מֵרְכָא סוֹף־פָּסוּק:

הָאֹמְרִים לְמַסֵּכָה אַתֶּם אֱלֹהֵינוּ:

וַתִּתְפַּלֵּל עַל־יְהוָֹה וּבָכֹה תִבְכֶּה:

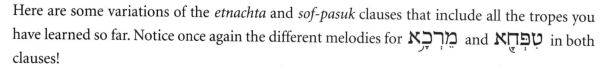

Here are some variations of the *etnachta* and *sof-pasuk* clauses that include all the tropes you have learned so far. Notice once again the different melodies for מֵרְכָא and טִפְחָא in both clauses!

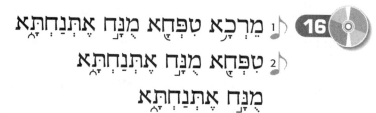

1 מֵרְכָא טִפְחָא מֻנָּח אֶתְנַחְתָּא

2 טִפְחָא מֻנָּח אֶתְנַחְתָּא

מֻנָּח אֶתְנַחְתָּא

5 מֵרְכָא טִפְחָא מֵרְכָא סוֹף־פָּסוּק:

6 טִפְחָא מֵרְכָא סוֹף־פָּסוּק:

8 טִפְחָא סוֹף־פָּסוּק:

7 מֵרְכָא טִפְחָא סוֹף־פָּסוּק:

מֵרְכָא סוֹף־פָּסוּק:

Once you know the סוֹף־פָּסוּק: clause, you can chant complete haftarah verses. Below are some examples. Don't forget to look ahead to find out if you are chanting an *etnachta* clause or a *sof-pasuk* clause. On the recording you will hear the tropes chanted first and then the words.

יְהֹוָה חָפֵץ לְמַעַן צִדְקוֹ יַגְדִּיל תּוֹרָה וְיַאְדִּיר:

Adonai is well pleased for the sake of His righteousness; God will magnify the Torah, and make it glorious. (Isaiah 42:21)

וַיֹּאמֶר יְהֹוָה לַדָּג וַיָּקֵא אֶת־יוֹנָה אֶל־הַיַּבָּשָׁה:

And *Adonai* spoke to the fish, and it vomited out Jonah onto the dry land. (Jonah 2:11)

וַיֵּרַע אֶל־יוֹנָה רָעָה גְדוֹלָה וַיִּחַר לוֹ:

And this displeased Jonah exceedingly, and he was very angry. (Jonah 4:1)

וְהִיא מָרַת נָפֶשׁ וַתִּתְפַּלֵּל עַל־יְהֹוָה וּבָכֹה תִבְכֶּה:

And she (Hannah) was in bitterness of soul, and prayed to *Adonai*, and wept bitterly. (1 Samuel 1:10)

יְהֹוָה מוֹרִישׁ וּמַעֲשִׁיר מַשְׁפִּיל אַף־מְרוֹמֵם:

Adonai makes poor and makes rich; The Eternal brings low and lifts up. (1 Samuel 2:7)

When you reach the final verse of a haftarah portion, the סוֹף־פָּסוּק: clause has a special melody. Here is what it sounds like:

מֵרְכָא טִפְּחָא מֵרְכָא סוֹף־פָּסוּק:

טִפְּחָא מֵרְכָא סוֹף־פָּסוּק:

מֵרְכָא טִפְּחָא סוֹף־פָּסוּק:

טִפְּחָא סוֹף־פָּסוּק:

צִיּוֹן בְּמִשְׁפָּט תִּפָּדֶה וְשָׁבֶיהָ בִּצְדָקָה:

Zion shall be redeemed with judgement, and those who return to her with righteousness. (Isaiah 1:27)

וַיֹּאמֶר לוֹ לֵךְ לְשָׁלוֹם וַיֵּלֶךְ מֵאִתּוֹ כִּבְרַת־אָרֶץ:

And he said to him, "Go in peace." So he departed from him some way. (2 Kings 5:19)

Congratulations! You are now ready to chant a section of your first haftarah.
The following text is found in 2 Samuel 22:33–40. This is the haftarah that accompanies the Torah portion *Ha-azinu*, from the Book of Deuteronomy. According to tradition, it is also read on the seventh day of Passover.

Treat the last verse as the end of your haftarah portion and use the special melody you just learned.

הָאֵל מָעוּזִּי חָיִל וַיַּתֵּר תָּמִים דַּרְכִּי: מְשַׁוֶּה רַגְלַי כָּאַיָּלוֹת וְעַל בָּמוֹתַי יַעֲמִדֵנִי: מְלַמֵּד יָדַי לַמִּלְחָמָה וְנִחַת קֶשֶׁת־נְחוּשָׁה זְרוֹעֹתָי: וַתִּתֶּן־לִי מָגֵן יִשְׁעֶךָ וַעֲנֹתְךָ תַּרְבֵּנִי: תַּרְחִיב צַעֲדִי תַחְתֵּנִי וְלֹא מָעֲדוּ קַרְסֻלָּי: אֶרְדְּפָה אֹיְבַי וָאַשְׁמִידֵם וְלֹא אָשׁוּב

עַד־כַּלּוֹתָם: וָאֲכַלֵּם וָאֶמְחָצֵם וְלֹא יְקוּמֻון וַיִּפְּלוּ תַּחַת רַגְלָי:
וַתַּזְרֵנִי חַיִל לַמִּלְחָמָה תַּכְרִיעַ קָמַי תַּחְתֵּנִי:

…[Who is…] the God who is my mighty shelter, who maps out for me a noble path, who has made my legs like a deer's, who makes me stand on the heights, who trains my hands for battle, my arms to bend a bow of bronze? You have bestowed on me Your triumphant shield, Your response [to me] enlarges [my strength]. You lengthen my stride, and my ankles do not waver. I chase my foes and destroy them, I do not turn back till they are no more. I destroy them; I shatter them; they cannot get up, they lie at my feet. You have girded me with strength for battle and laid low my foes beneath me. (2 Samuel 22:33–40)

How Cantillation Works

You have mastered two clauses in our system of haftarah chanting—the *etnachta* clause and the *sof-pasuk* clause. The אֶתְנַחְתָּא and those tropes that lead up to it bring a verse of the haftarah to a significant but not final pause. The סוֹף־פָּסוּק: and those tropes that lead up to it bring a verse to an end, as in the following example:

$$וְהִיא מָרַת נָפֶשׁ$$

And she [Hannah] was in bitterness of soul,

$$וַתִּתְפַּלֵּל עַל־יְהֹוָה וּבָכֹה תִבְכֶּה:$$

And prayed to *Adonai*, and wept bitterly. (1 Samuel 1:10)

Thus the אֶתְנַחְתָּא functions as the main divider of the sentence: sometimes it is like a comma, and sometimes it is like a semicolon. The סוֹף־פָּסוּק: is definitely a period. Besides these two separators, we need more ways to subdivide the sentences in the text appropriately—to indicate commas (since there can be more than one in a sentence), dashes, and other points of inflection. Consequently you will learn four more clauses, making a total of six. Once you have mastered the six clauses—and you already know two—you will be able to chant haftarah.

The six trope clauses may be thought of as six families of tropes. Each family has a "head" trope with which the clause will always end. Within each clause are other tropes with varying degrees of "pausal power." These tropes can be divided into two groups:

- The tropes that indicate a pause in the flow of text are called "separators" or מַפְסִיקִים (*mafsikim*; singular: מַפְסִיק, *mafsik*). These are also known as "disjunctives" or "lords."
- In contrast, some tropes have no pausal power at all but flow right into the next trope. We call these tropes "connectors" or מְחַבְּרִים (*m'chabrim*; singular: מְחַבֵּר, *m'chaber*). They are also known as "conjunctives" or "servants."

The "head" trope is always the strongest מַפְסִיק in any clause and gives the clause its name. The rest of the clause may include both מַפְסִיקִים and מְחַבְּרִים. When a מְחַבֵּר comes just before a מַפְסִיק, it "serves" the מַפְסִיק. מַפְסִיקִים, such as אֶתְנַחְתָּא, סוֹף־פָּסוּק:, and טִפְחָא, function as separators between clauses. Their separating power is not equal: סוֹף־פָּסוּק is stronger than אֶתְנַחְתָּא, and אֶתְנַחְתָּא in turn is stronger than טִפְחָא. Take another look at that verse of haftarah:

וְהִיא מָרַת נָפֶשׁ
וַתִּתְפַּלֵּל עַל־יְהוָֹה וּבָכֹה תִבְכֶּה:

This verse contains two clauses: an *etnachta* clause ending with the word נָפֶשׁ, and a *sof-pasuk* clause ending with the word תִבְכֶּה:. The first clause contains three words with three tropes. The first trope, טִפְחָא, is considered a מַפְסִיק with moderate pausal power. The second trope, מֻנָּח, is a מְחַבֵּר that flows directly into the third trope, אֶתְנַחְתָּא. The second clause contains five words with four tropes. The first trope, מֵרְכָא, is a מְחַבֵּר that flows directly into the מַפְסִיק, which in this case is טִפְחָא. Then follows another מֵרְכָא that serves the סוֹף־פָּסוּק: on the last word.

When the verse is notated in English, it looks like this:

And she (Hannah),   was in bitterness of soul,   and prayed to *Adonai*,   and wept bitterly.

When you chant it, you make a slight pause after וְהִיא, a longer pause after נָפֶשׁ, and a clear stop after the final word of the verse, תִבְכֶּה:. The second and fourth words should flow without a pause into the next words, which they serve.

וְהִיא מָרַת נָפֶשׁ
וַתִּתְפַּלֵּל עַל־יְהוָֹה וּבָכֹה תִבְכֶּה:

Here is a review of all the possible combinations in the two trope clauses you've learned so far:

Etnachta Clause מַעֲרֶכֶת אֶתְנַחְתָּא

אֶתְנַחְתָּא מֻנַּח מֵרְכָא טִפְחָא מֵרְכָא

אֶתְנַחְתָּא מֻנַּח טִפְחָא

אֶתְנַחְתָּא מֻנַּח

אֶתְנַחְתָּא מֵרְכָא טִפְחָא

אֶתְנַחְתָּא טִפְחָא

אֶתְנַחְתָּא

Sof-Pasuk Clause מַעֲרֶכֶת סוֹף־פָּסוּק

סוֹף־פָּסוּק: מֵרְכָא טִפְחָא מֵרְכָא

סוֹף־פָּסוּק: מֵרְכָא טִפְחָא

סוֹף־פָּסוּק: טִפְחָא

סוֹף־פָּסוּק: מֵרְכָא טִפְחָא

סוֹף־פָּסוּק: מֵרְכָא

סוֹף־פָּסוּק:

LESSON 4

The *Katon* Clause · מַעֲרֶכֶת קָטֹן

This trope clause concludes with the קָטֹן (katon), which consists of two dots vertically arranged and placed over the first letter of a word's accented syllable:

קָטֹן is the first of several tropes you will learn that are notated *above* the first letter of the word's accented syllable. You may hear other people refer to katon as *zakef-katon, zakef-katan,* or just *zakef.* Although all these terms are correct, in the following pages we will use the term קָטֹן. When we hear the word קָטֹן, we are likely to think of the Hebrew word קָטָן, meaning "small." Although the dots are small, they are powerful!

קָטֹן is a מַפְסִיק that brings to a temporary halt an important phrase within a verse of haftarah. Here are some examples:

וָאוֹלֵךְ אֶתְכֶם בַּמִּדְבָּר אַרְבָּעִים שָׁנָה

…and led you through the wilderness for forty **years**

לָרֶשֶׁת אֶת־אֶרֶץ הָאֱמֹרִי:

…to possess the land of the Amorite. (Amos 2:10)

וַיְזוֹרֵר הַנַּעַר עַד־שֶׁבַע פְּעָמִים

…and the child sneezed seven **times**,

וַיִּפְקַח הַנַּעַר אֶת־עֵינָיו:

and the child opened his eyes. (2 Kings 4:35)

קָטֹן sounds like this:

The chant goes up and down, bringing the phrase to a temporary halt within the verse.[4]

---

[4] The more tropes you know, the more you realize that some may have gotten their shape from the direction of their musical phrase. Originally, long before tropes were written down, readers of the Torah and haftarah were reminded of the melodies by hand signals. This method of music teaching is called *cheironomy,* a Greek term that means "teaching melody with one's hands." In some Jewish communities, this system is still in use.

Practice the following words with קָטֹן:

קָטֹן **21**

עֲבָדוּ

עַמּוֹ

הָעוֹלָם

טוֹבִים

אַל־תַּחְשֹׁךְ

נִינְוֵה

An important servant or helper of קָטֹן—that is, a trope that leads us to it—is פַּשְׁטָא (*pashta*):

This very common trope is the first of several you will learn that are always notated *above the final letter of a word*. These tropes are called "postpositive."

פַּשְׁטָא **always appears above a word's final letter.**

It sounds almost the way it looks, starting low and jumping up, like this: פַּשְׁטָא **22**

Practice the following words with פַּשְׁטָא:

פַּשְׁטָא

בָּחַר

בַּתּוֹרָה

עִמָּהֶם

בְּגָרוֹן

הַדָּבָר

The "over-the-last-letter" rule about פַּשְׁטָא presents an interesting problem that you may have already anticipated. One of the fundamental purposes of cantillation is, of course, to indicate the accented syllable. If a פַּשְׁטָא word is accented on the last syllable—like most Hebrew words—there is no problem. But what if a word is accented on a different syllable, like the word עַיִן or הַנַּעַר? In that case, you will see the פַּשְׁטָא symbol twice: over the final letter of the word to indicate that it is indeed a פַּשְׁטָא, and also over the accented syllable, like this: עַיִן or הַנַּעַר.

If a word is accented not on the last syllable but on a different syllable, you will see the פַּשְׁטָא symbol twice.

Here are some examples. After you try to chant each word, listen to the recording to hear if you did it correctly.

23 פַּשְׁטָא
אֱלֹהֵינוּ
הַנַּעַר
מַיִם
וַיָּקָם

Practice the following combinations of פַּשְׁטָא and קָטֹן:

24 13 פַּשְׁטָא קָטֹן
בְּגָרוֹן אַל־תֵּחָשׁ
מַיִם עַד־נָפֶשׁ
וַיָּקָם מִכִּסְאוֹ

פַּשְׁטָא is often preceded by מַהְפָּךְ (*mapach*). מַהְפָּךְ looks somewhat like the arithmetic sign for "less than" and is always notated beneath a word:

מְהֻפָּךְ is a מְחַבֵּר and functions as a connector, or servant, just like מֻנָּח.

It sounds like this:

מְהֻפָּךְ **25**

Try the following examples:

מְהֻפָּךְ
אַתָּה
אֲשֶׁר
הַבּוֹחֵר
קָרָא
לָבוֹא

Given that מְהֻפָּךְ and פַּשְׁטָא enjoy such a close relationship, you should not be surprised to learn that פַּשְׁטָא begins on the same note on which מְהֻפָּךְ ends:

מְהֻפָּךְ ◄ פַּשְׁטָא **26**
אַתָּה יְיָ
אֲשֶׁר בָּחַר
הַבּוֹחֵר בַּתּוֹרָה
לָבוֹא עִמָּהֶם
קָרָא בְּגָרוֹן

With מְהֻפָּךְ – פַּשְׁטָא – קָטֹן, you have almost mastered the *katon* clause. The following examples from the haftarah include these three tropes, as well as a review of the earlier tropes you have learned.

מְהֻפָּךְ פַּשְׁטָא קָטֹן ₁₁ **27**

לָבוֹא עִמָּהֶם תַּרְשִׁישָׁה

...to go with them to Tarshish... (Jonah 1:3)

קְרָא בְגָרוֹן אַל־תַּחְשֹׂךְ כַּשׁוֹפָר הָרֵם קוֹלֶךָ
וְהַגֵּד לְעַמִּי פִּשְׁעָם וּלְבֵית יַעֲקֹב חַטֹּאתָם:

Cry aloud, spare not, lift up your voice like a shofar, and show My people their transgression, and the house of Jacob their sins. (Isaiah 58:1)

אֲפָפוּנִי מַיִם עַד־נֶפֶשׁ תְּהוֹם יְסֹבְבֵנִי סוּף חָבוּשׁ לְרֹאשִׁי:

The waters surrounded me, even to the soul; the depth closed around me, the weeds were wrapped around my head. (Jonah 2:6)

You need to learn—or, more accurately, relearn—one more trope in order to complete your understanding of the *katon* clause. This trope is one that you already know. It is the trope called מֻנָּח (*munach*)—the one that is shaped like a right angle. Although the word מֻנָּח comes from the root "to rest," it is a trope that *never* rests! מֻנָּח is the ultimate connector or servant. It serves אֶתְנַחְתָּא, as we learned earlier. It also serves קָטֹן and other tropes.

The melody of מֻנָּח changes, depending on the trope that follows it.

Our understanding of מֻנָּח leads us to an important generalization about the melodic patterns of the tropes:

The melody of the מַפְסִיקִים (separators) is constant, while the melody of some מְחַבְּרִים (connectors) varies.

Before קָטֹן, the melody of מֻנָּח goes down and then up a little higher, leading into קָטֹן. Try to sing each phrase below, then listen and repeat each one:

מֻנָּח קָטֹן **28**
מֶלֶךְ הָעוֹלָם
בִּנְבִיאִים טוֹבִים
וּבְמֹשֶׁה עַבְדּוֹ
וּבְיִשְׂרָאֵל עַמּוֹ

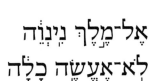

אֶל־מֶ֣לֶךְ נִֽינְוֵֽה

לֹא־אֶעֱשֶׂ֖ה כָּלָֽה

When מֻנַּח and קָטֹן (or any other two trope marks) appear in a single word, simply chant them on their respective syllables. Try these examples:

מֻנַּח קָטֹן **28**

וּפָרָשִׁ֗ים

מְשֻׁבָתָ֑ם

וְאָנֹכִֽי

The following are the most common variations of מַעֲרֶכֶת קָטֹן, the *katon* clause:

קָטֹן מֻנַּח פַּשְׁטָא ◄ מַהְפָּךְ ♪₁₀ **29**

קָטֹן פַּשְׁטָא ◄ מַהְפָּךְ ♪₁₁

קָטֹן מֻנַּח פַּשְׁטָא ♪₁₂

קָטֹן מֻנַּח ♪

קָטֹן פַּשְׁטָא ♪₁₃

The following examples from haftarah and the blessing before it use all the tropes you have learned so far. As the examples get longer, you may wish to break down each one into its various clauses and practice it in the following way:

Find the trope that gives each clause its name (e.g., *sof-pasuk, etnachta, katon*). Each of these tropes marks the end of a clause. For each clause:

1. Read the Hebrew words.
2. Chant the tropes, using their names.
3. Chant the actual text.

When you have done these steps, put all the clauses together and chant the entire example.

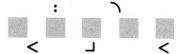

אֲשֶׁר בָּחַר בִּנְבִיאִים טוֹבִים וְרָצָה בְדִבְרֵיהֶם הַנֶּאֱמָרִים בֶּאֱמֶת

…who has chosen faithful prophets to speak words of truth… (blessing)

הַבּוֹחֵר בַּתּוֹרָה וּבְמֹשֶׁה עַבְדּוֹ וּבְיִשְׂרָאֵל עַמּוֹ וּבִנְבִיאֵי הָאֱמֶת
וָצֶדֶק:

…for the revelation of Torah, for Moses, God's servant and Israel, God's people, and for the prophets of truth and righteousness. (blessing)

וַיִּגַּע הַדָּבָר אֶל־מֶלֶךְ נִינְוֵה וַיָּקָם מִכִּסְאוֹ וַיַּעֲבֵר אַדַּרְתּוֹ מֵעָלָיו
וַיְכַס שַׂק וַיֵּשֶׁב עַל־הָאֵפֶר:

And word came to the king of Nineveh, and he arose from his throne, and he took off his robe, and covered himself with sackcloth, and sat in ashes. (Jonah 3:6)

אֲפָפוּנִי מַיִם עַד־נֶפֶשׁ תְּהוֹם יְסֹבְבֵנִי סוּף חָבוּשׁ לְרֹאשִׁי:

The waters surrounded me, even to the soul; the depth closed around me, the weeds were wrapped around my head. (Jonah 2:6)

וְאֹתְךָ לֹא־אֶעֱשֶׂה כָלָה וְיִסַּרְתִּיךָ לַמִּשְׁפָּט וְנַקֵּה לֹא אֲנַקֶּךָ:

… I will not make a full end of you, but correct you in due measure; yet I will not leave you unpunished. (Jeremiah 46:28)

There is a trope that looks just like מַהְפַּךְ but is called יְתִיב (*y'tiv*):

Although it looks similar, its function and sound are very different. Here are some ways to tell the two tropes apart:

1. יְתִיב appears only when the first word of the clause is stressed on the first syllable.
2. It always appears underneath the first letter of the word *and a little to the right*.
3. It is always followed by קָטֹן or מְנֻחַ קָטֹן (whereas מַהְפַּךְ is always followed by פַּשְׁטָא).

Here is how יְתִיב sounds:

יְתִיב **31**

Try the following examples of *katon* clauses with the trope יְתִיב:

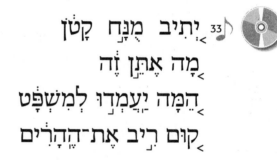

33

יְתִיב מְנֻחַ קָטֹן

מָה אֶתֶּן זֶה

הֵמָּה יַעַמְדוּ לְמִשְׁפָּט

קוּם רִיב אֶת־הֶהָרִים

34

יְתִיב קָטֹן

שׁוּבָה יִשְׂרָאֵל

אַף בַּל־זֹרָעוּ

Now practice the following phrases that include *katon* clauses with the trope יְתִיב:

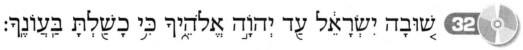

שׁוּבָה יִשְׂרָאֵל עַד יְהֹוָה אֱלֹהֶיךָ כִּי כָשַׁלְתָּ בַּעֲוֹנֶךָ: **32**

O Israel, return to *Adonai*, your God; for you have stumbled in your iniquity. (Hosea 14:2)

מָה אֶתֶּן זֶה לִפְנֵי מֵאָה אִישׁ

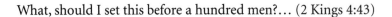

What, should I set this before a hundred men?... (2 Kings 4:43)

הֵ֡מָּה יַעַמְד֣וּ לְמִשְׁפָּט֮ בְּמִשְׁפָּטַ֣י יִשְׁפְּט֒הוּ
וְאֶת־תּוֹרֹתַ֣י וְאֶת־חֻקֹּתַי֙ בְּכָל־מוֹעֲדַ֣י יִשְׁמֹ֔רוּ
וְאֶת־שַׁבְּתוֹתַ֖י יְקַדֵּֽשׁוּ׃

...they act as judges; and they shall judge it according to My judgments; and they shall keep
My laws and My statutes in all My appointed times; and they shall sanctify My Sabbaths.
(Ezekiel 44:24)

כִּ֥י לֹֽא־יָדַ֣ע מָנ֔וֹחַ כִּֽי־מַלְאַ֥ךְ יְהֹוָ֖ה הֽוּא׃

...For Manoah knew not that he was an angel of _Adonai_. (Judges 13:16)

ק֚וּם רִ֣יב אֶת־הֶֽהָרִ֔ים וְתִשְׁמַ֥עְנָה הַגְּבָע֖וֹת קוֹלֶֽךָ׃

...Arise, contend before the mountains, and let the hills hear your voice. (Micah 6:1)

Congratulations! You have now mastered three of the six clauses in the cantillation of haftarah
and have learned nine tropes. These clauses and tropes cover about three-quarters of the text of
the haftarah.

A Look at *Kadma* • קַדְמָא

When you first look at the trope קַדְמָא (*kadma*), you may notice that it looks exactly like פַּשְׁטָא (*pashta*). Therefore, before you begin to use this trope, let's learn how to distinguish it from its twin. Although the two may look identical, they are fundamentally different in character and purpose.

The first difference is their placement on a word. You will recall that פַּשְׁטָא always appears above the final letter of a word. Therefore, if a trope that looks exactly like פַּשְׁטָא is notated above another letter, it is not a פַּשְׁטָא but a קַדְמָא. קַדְמָא, like most tropes, is notated above the first letter of a word's accented syllable.

For example: (קַדְמָא)   אֲשֶׁר

(פַּשְׁטָא)   אֲשֶׁר

More important, however, is the contrast in the way the two tropes function. פַּשְׁטָא is a מַפְסִיק. It brings a short phrase within a *katon* clause to a temporary pause, as in the following examples:

תּוֹרַת אֱמֶת\ הָיְתָה בְּפִיהוּ

The Torah of **truth** / was in his mouth… (Malachi 2:6)

אֲפָפוּנִי מַיִם\ עַד־נֶפֶשׁ תְּהוֹם יְסֹבְבֵנִי

I was surrounded by **waters** / even to the soul; the depth closed around me… (Jonah 2:6)

קַדְמָא, on the other hand, is a מְחַבֵּר. It leads us to the next word in the text:

וָאוֹלֵךְ אֶתְכֶם בַּמִּדְבָּר אַרְבָּעִים שָׁנָה\
לָרֶשֶׁת אֶת־אֶרֶץ הָאֱמֹרִי:

…**and led you** forty years through the wilderness / to possess the land of the Amorite.
(Amos 2:10)

הִנֵּה אֲנִי לֹקֵחַ אֶת־בְּנֵי יִשְׂרָאֵל \ מִבֵּין הַגּוֹיִם אֲשֶׁר הָלְכוּ־שָׁם

...**Behold,** I will take the people of Israel / from among the nations, where they have gone...(Ezekiel 37:21)

When קַדְמָא serves מַהְפַּךְ, that is, when it immediately precedes מַהְפַּךְ, its melody has just two notes, the second higher than the first and leading right into מַהְפַּךְ:

קַדְמָא

קַדְמָא ◄ מַהְפַּךְ

Practice the following combinations from the haftarah:

קַדְמָא ◄ מַהְפַּךְ

בָּרוּךְ אַתָּה

הִנֵּה אֲנִי

אֲשֶׁר מָלַךְ

וָאוֹלֵךְ אֶתְכֶם

Now, for more of a challenge, practice some longer phrases from haftarah that utilize all the tropes you have learned so far. Be sure to notice the difference between פַּשְׁטָא and קַדְמָא. It is helpful to chant the tropes alone first and then chant the text.

בָּרוּךְ אַתָּה יְיָ אֱלֹהֵינוּ מֶלֶךְ הָעוֹלָם אֲשֶׁר בָּחַר בִּנְבִיאִים טוֹבִים וְרָצָה בְדִבְרֵיהֶם הַנֶּאֱמָרִים בֶּאֱמֶת

Blessed is *Adonai*, our God, Sovereign of the universe, who has chosen faithful prophets to speak words of truth... (blessing before the reading of the haftarah)

וָאוֹלֵךְ אֶתְכֶם בַּמִּדְבָּר אַרְבָּעִים שָׁנָה לָרֶשֶׁת אֶת־אֶרֶץ הָאֱמֹרִי:

...who led you forty years through the wilderness, to possess the land of the Amorite. (Amos 2:10)

הִנֵּה אֲנִי לֹקֵחַ אֶת־בְּנֵי יִשְׂרָאֵל מִבֵּין הַגּוֹיִם אֲשֶׁר הָלְכוּ־שָׁם

Behold, I will take the people of Israel from among the nations, where they have gone…
(Ezekiel 37:21)

אֲשֶׁר מָלַךְ דָּוִד עַל־יִשְׂרָאֵל אַרְבָּעִים שָׁנָה
בְּחֶבְרוֹן מָלַךְ שֶׁבַע שָׁנִים וּבִירוּשָׁלַם מָלַךְ שְׁלֹשִׁים
וְשָׁלֹשׁ שָׁנִים:

…David reigned over Israel [for] forty years; seven years he reigned in Hebron, and thirty-three years he reigned in Jerusalem. (1 Kings 2:11)

כִּרְאוֹת אִישׁ־הָאֱלֹהִים אֹתָהּ מִנֶּגֶד וַיֹּאמֶר אֶל־גֵּיחֲזִי נַעֲרוֹ הִנֵּה
הַשּׁוּנַמִּית הַלָּז:

…When the man of God saw her far away, he said to Gehazi his servant, "Behold, yonder is that Shunammite." (2 Kings 4:25)

מַהְפָּךְ may also be preceded by a מֻנַּח. As you know, מֻנַּח is chanted differently depending on which trope it serves. Here, the מֻנַּח melody leads directly into the מַהְפָּךְ:

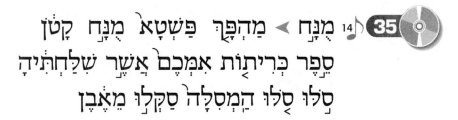

You may find the following four-step process useful in preparing a longer section of haftarah, such as the two texts that follow on pages 34–35. The first, Isaiah 41:7–10, is from *Haftarat Lech L'cha*. The second selection is from the haftarah of Yom Kippur afternoon, the Book of Jonah.

1. Read the words and make sure that you are comfortable with the Hebrew text.
2. Next separate the words according to the trope clauses. The most important break in the first verse is, of course, the last word יִמּוֹט:, with the trope סוֹף־פָּסוּק:. The next most important separator is the אֶתְנַחְתָּא on the word פָּעַם. Now the קָטֹן on the word אֶת־צֹרֵף and the קָטֹן on the word הוּא indicate that the verse has four distinct clauses:

וַיְחַזֵּק חָרָשׁ אֶת־צֹרֵף

מַחֲלִיק פַּטִּישׁ אֶת־הוֹלֶם פָּעַם

אֹמֵר לַדֶּבֶק טוֹב הוּא

וַיְחַזְּקֵהוּ בְמַסְמְרִים לֹא יִמּוֹט:

3. Now try to chant the tropes in each clause:

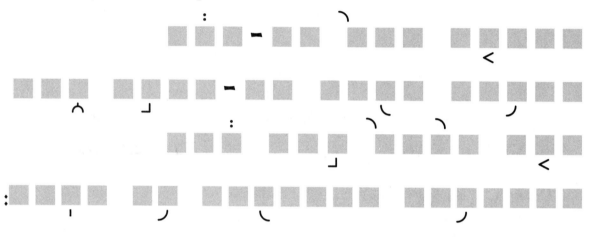

4. Finally, chant the words, pausing slightly at קָטֹן and a little more after אֶתְנַחְתָּא.

This four-step process will help you prepare your haftarah reading in a methodical manner and will ensure that you are comfortable with all aspects of the portion. The more you read haftarah, the sooner you will go on "automatic pilot," and the basic reading and discerning of trope relationships will come instinctively. With practice, you will within a short time be able to "sight-read" a verse from the haftarah!

Now try the next few verses on your own:

וַיְחַזֵּק חָרָשׁ אֶת־צֹרֵף מַחֲלִיק פַּטִּישׁ אֶת־הוֹלֶם פָּעַם אֹמֵר

לַדֶּבֶק טוֹב הוּא וַיְחַזְּקֵהוּ בְמַסְמְרִים לֹא יִמּוֹט: וְאַתָּה יִשְׂרָאֵל

עַבְדִּי יַעֲקֹב אֲשֶׁר בְּחַרְתִּיךָ זֶרַע אַבְרָהָם אֹהֲבִי: אֲשֶׁר

הֶחֱזַקְתִּיךָ מִקְצוֹת הָאָרֶץ וּמֵאֲצִילֶיהָ קְרָאתִיךָ וָאֹמַר לְךָ

עַבְדִּי־אַתָּה בְּחַרְתִּיךָ וְלֹא מְאַסְתִּיךָ: אַל־תִּירָא כִּי עִמְּךָ־אָנִי

אַל־תִּשְׁתָּע כִּי־אֲנִי אֱלֹהֶיךָ אִמַּצְתִּיךְ אַף־עֲזַרְתִּיךְ אַף־
תְּמַכְתִּיךְ בִּימִין צִדְקִי:

The artisan encourages the goldsmith. The one who hammers the metal smooth compliments the one who strikes the anvil, saying, "The soldering is good," and they fasten it in place with nails: it cannot be moved. But you, Israel, My servant, Jacob, My chosen one, offspring of Abraham, My friend—I have taken hold of you from the ends of the earth, and called you from its far corners; and said to you: You are My servant, I have chosen you, and not rejected you. Have no fear, for I am with you; do not be afraid, for I am your God; I will give you strength, I will help you, I will uphold you with My victorious hand. (Isaiah 41:7–10)

וַתַּשְׁלִיכֵנִי מְצוּלָה בִּלְבַב יַמִּים וְנָהָר יְסֹבְבֵנִי כָּל־מִשְׁבָּרֶיךָ
וְגַלֶּיךָ עָלַי עָבָרוּ: וַאֲנִי אָמַרְתִּי נִגְרַשְׁתִּי מִנֶּגֶד עֵינֶיךָ אַךְ אוֹסִיף
לְהַבִּיט אֶל־הֵיכַל קָדְשֶׁךָ: אֲפָפוּנִי מַיִם עַד־נֶפֶשׁ תְּהוֹם יְסֹבְבֵנִי
סוּף חָבוּשׁ לְרֹאשִׁי:

For You cast me into the deep, in the heart of the seas; and the floods surrounded me; all Your billows and Your waves passed over me. Then I said, "I am cast out from Your presence; yet I will look again toward Your holy temple. The waters surrounded me, even to the soul; the depth closed around me, the weeds were wrapped around my head." (Jonah 2:4–6)

LESSON 6

Zakef Gadol · זָקֵף גָּדוֹל

זָקֵף גָּדוֹל (zakef gadol) functions as a separator, just like קָטֹן ([zakef] katon). In fact, some people consider it to be a substitute for a *katon* clause. It generally stands on its own and is easy to recognize: a vertical line flanked by two vertical dots on its right, *above* the first letter of a word's stressed syllable:

It sounds like this:

זָקֵף גָּדוֹל **38**

Practice this trope a number of times:

זָקֵף גָּדוֹל **32** ♪
וּגְאָלוֹ
בֶּעָשֹׂרִי
בֶּן־אָדָם
נָשִׁים

Chant the following phrases from *N'vi-im* that include זָקֵף גָּדוֹל:

39

כִּי־פָדָה יְהֹוָה אֶת־יַעֲקֹב וּגְאָלוֹ מִיַּד חָזָק מִמֶּנּוּ:

For *Adonai* has redeemed Jacob, and ransomed him from the hand of him who was stronger than he. (Jeremiah 31:11)

בַּשָּׁנָה הָעֲשִׂירִית בָּעֲשִׂרִי בִּשְׁנֵים עָשָׂר לַחֹדֶשׁ הָיָה
דְבַר־יְהֹוָה אֵלַי לֵאמֹר:

In the tenth year, in the tenth month, in the twelfth day of the month, the word of *Adonai* came to me, saying: (Ezekiel 29:1)

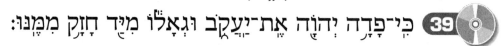

בֶּן־אָדָ֗ם שִׂ֤ים פָּנֶ֙יךָ֙ עַל־פַּרְעֹ֣ה מֶ֣לֶךְ מִצְרָ֑יִם וְהִנָּבֵ֥א עָלָ֖יו
וְעַל־מִצְרַ֥יִם כֻּלָּֽהּ׃

Son of man, set your face against Pharaoh, king of Egypt, and prophesy against him, and against all Egypt. (Ezekiel 29:2)

בִּיבֹ֤שׁ קְצִירָהּ֙ תִּשָּׁבַ֔רְנָה נָשִׁים֙ בָּא֣וֹת מְאִיר֣וֹת אוֹתָ֑הּ כִּ֣י לֹ֤א
עַם־בִּינוֹת֙ ה֔וּא עַל־כֵּן֙ לֹֽא־יְרַחֲמֶ֣נּוּ עֹשֵׂ֔הוּ וְיֹצְר֖וֹ לֹ֥א יְחֻנֶּֽנּוּ׃

When the crown withers, they crack; women come and use them to kindle fires. Since this people has no understanding, their Maker will show them no pity, their Creator will show them no mercy. (Isaiah 27:11)

The *T'vir* Clause • מַעֲרֶכֶת תְּבִיר

תְּבִיר looks like a *mercha* with a dot inside it:

It is a מַפְסִיק and temporarily stops the thought within a verse, as in the following example:

וַיִּרָא דָוִד / אֶת־יְהֹוָה בַּיֹּום הַהוּא // וַיֹּאמֶר / אֵיךְ / יָבֹוא אֵלַי אֲרֹון יְהֹוָה:

And feared **David** *Adonai* that day, and said, "**How** shall the ark of *Adonai* come to me?" (2 Samuel 6:9)

Here are some words that feature תְּבִיר:

תְּבִיר
תָּמִיד
קָדֹושׁ
שִׁפְחָתְךָ
וְשָׁלֵשׁ

Frequently תְּבִיר is preceded by a trope called דַּרְגָּא (*darga*). דַּרְגָּא is a מְחַבֵּר and looks like a backward *z* (some editions of *Tanach* use a backward *s*):

As you listen to דַּרְגָּא, you will note that this trope first goes up and then descends—step by step:

דַּרְגָּא

Try the following examples:

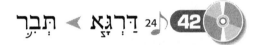

דַּרְגָּא **41**

קָדוֹשׁ

תִּמְצָא

שְׁעָרֶיךָ

עֶשְׂרִים

תְּבִיר starts on the same note on which דַּרְגָּא ended:

תְּבַר ◄ דַּרְגָּא ♩24 **42**

Practice the examples below:

שְׁעָרֶיךָ תָּמִיד

קָדוֹשׁ קָדוֹשׁ

תִּמְצָא שִׁפְחָתֶךָ

עֶשְׂרִים וְשָׁלֹשׁ

When the melody of a trope ends by going up, as it does with תְּבִיר, and the accent falls before the last syllable, it is necessary to repeat the last note of the melody for the last syllable of the word. In other words, the main melodic motif is sung on the accented syllable.

Try these examples:

תְּבִיר **43**

וּבְטֶרֶם

עֵגֶל

תְּבִיר may also be preceded by מֵרְכָא, the same trope that preceded טִפְחָא. But מֵרְכָא, a connector, is chanted differently before תְּבִיר: It sounds like the first, second, and last note of the דַּרְגָּא without the in-between notes:

מֵרְכָא 25 44

Listen to and then chant each of the following examples:

23 תְּבִיר

24 דַּרְגָּא ◄ תְּבִיר

25 מֵרְכָא ◄ תְּבִיר

מֵרְכָא ◄ תְּבִיר 45

וַיִּרָא דָוִד

יִרְעֶה עֵגֶל

חֵרֵף נַפְשׁוֹ

Either דַּרְגָּא תְּבִר or מֵרְכָא תְּבִיר can be preceded by קַדְמָא or מֵנַח.

The קַדְמָא before מֵרְכָא תְּבִיר or דַּרְגָּא תְּבִר sounds exactly like the קַדְמָא before מַהְפָּךְ. It also ends on the same note on which מֵרְכָא and דַּרְגָּא start.

Here are some combinations:

26 קַדְמָא ◄ דַּרְגָּא ◄ תְּבִיר 46

וּפִתְּחוּ שְׁעָרַיִךְ תָּמִיד

בִּשְׁנַת עֶשְׂרִים וְשָׁלֹשׁ

27 קַדְמָא ◄ מֵרְכָא ◄ תְּבִיר

אֲשֶׁר נָתַן לָכֶם

וְלֹא־קָמָה עוֹד רוּחַ

מְנָח before דַּרְגָּא תְּבִיר or מֵרְכָא תְּבִיר begins high, jumps down, then goes back up.
Listen:

מְנָח **47**

Practice the following examples of the various combinations:

מְנָח ◄ דַּרְגָּא ◄ תְּבִיר **28**

אֶת אֲשֶׁר יוֹרִישֶׁךָ

מְנָח ◄ מֵרְכָא ◄ תְּבִיר

עַם חֵרֵף נַפְשׁוֹ

שָׁם יִרְעֶה עֵגֶל

When you are ready to chant some text, try the following passages. Remember to follow the
four-step process outlined in lesson 5.

וְקָרָא זֶה אֶל־זֶה וְאָמַר קָדוֹשׁ קָדוֹשׁ קָדוֹשׁ יְהוָה צְבָאוֹת **48**
מְלֹא כָל־הָאָרֶץ כְּבוֹדוֹ:

And each called to the other: "Holy, holy, holy is the God of heaven's hosts, whose Presence
fills all the earth!" (Isaiah 6:3)

וּפִתְּחוּ שְׁעָרַיִךְ תָּמִיד יוֹמָם וָלַיְלָה לֹא יִסָּגֵרוּ
לְהָבִיא אֵלַיִךְ חֵיל גּוֹיִם וּמַלְכֵיהֶם נְהוּגִים:

Therefore your gates shall be open continually; they shall not be closed day or night; that
men may bring to you the wealth of the nations, with their kings led in procession. (Isaiah
60:11)

עַם חֵרֵף נַפְשׁוֹ לָמוּת וְנַפְתָּלִי עַל מְרוֹמֵי שָׂדֶה:

...a people who risked their lives to the death, and Naphtali likewise, on the high places of
the field. (Judges 5:18)

בִּשְׁנַ֣ת עֶשְׂרִ֤ים וְשָׁלֹשׁ֙ שָׁנָ֔ה לַמֶּ֖לֶךְ יְהוֹאָ֑שׁ
לֹא־חִזְּק֥וּ הַכֹּהֲנִ֖ים אֶת־בֶּ֥דֶק הַבָּֽיִת׃

...In the twenty third year of King Jehoash the priests had not repaired the breaches of the House. (2 Kings 12:7)

וַתֹּ֗אמֶר תִּמְצָ֧א שִׁפְחָתְךָ֛ חֵ֖ן בְּעֵינֶ֑יךָ
וַתֵּ֨לֶךְ הָאִשָּׁ֤ה לְדַרְכָּהּ֙ וַתֹּאכַ֔ל וּפָנֶ֥יהָ לֹא־הָֽיוּ־לָ֖הּ עֽוֹד׃

And she said, Let your maidservant find grace in your sight. So the woman went her way, and ate, and her countenance was sad no more. (1 Samuel 1:18)

שָׁ֣ם יִרְעֶ֥ה עֵ֖גֶל וְשָׁ֣ם יִרְבָּ֑ץ וְכִלָּ֖ה סְעִפֶֽיהָ׃

...there shall the calf feed, and there shall he lie down, and consume its branches. (Isaiah 27:10)

There is one occasion on which the trope מֵרְכָא כְּפוּלָה (mercha-k'fulah) takes the place of תְּבִיר, and that is in *Haftarat B'ha-alot'cha*. מֵרְכָא כְּפוּלָה (double *mercha*) looks like two *mercha*s, one nestled within the other:

It is chanted as a short four-note scale, going up and then down, starting on the last note of דַּרְגָּא:

מֵרְכָא כְּפוּלָה is preceded by דַּרְגָּא and followed by טִפְחָא:

דַּרְגָּא ‹ מֵרְכָא כְּפוּלָה ‹ טִפְחָא

Chant the following example:

הֲל֨וֹא זֶ֥ה א֛וּד מֻצָּ֖ל מֵאֵֽשׁ׃

...Is not this a brand plucked out of the fire? (Zechariah 3:2)

LESSON 8

The *R'vi-i* Clause • מַעֲרֶכֶת רְבִיעִי

Part One

The Hebrew word רְבִיעִי (*r'vi-i*) means "fourth" (from the word אַרְבַּע, "four") and the diamond-shaped trope רְבִיעִי has four sides:[5]

רְבִיעִי is a מַפְסִיק and sounds like this:

Chant the following words with רְבִיעִי:

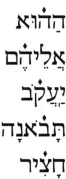

הַהוּא
אֲלֵיהֶם
יַעֲקֹב
תְּבֹאנָה
חָצִיר

While רְבִיעִי can stand alone, it is more often accompanied by its servant מֻנַּח. Yes, this is the same מֻנַּח that served אֶתְנַחְתָּא and קָטֹן. Recall, however, that מֻנַּח is one of those connectors whose melody changes depending on which trope follows it. Its melody before רְבִיעִי is quite different from that before אֶתְנַחְתָּא or קָטֹן. Here, it ascends, descends, and leads into רְבִיעִי.

Listen:

מֻנַּח ◄ רְבִיעִי 18 **51**

Now chant the following examples:

מֻנַּח ◄ רְבִיעִי
שְׁאֵרִית יַעֲקֹב

---

[5] In some editions of *Tanach*, the רְבִיעִי may look more like a circle than a diamond.

וַיֹּאמֶר אֲלֵיהֶם
בַּיֹּום הַהוּא
אָז תָּבֹאנָה

There is a special trope that often precedes מֻנַּח רְבִיעִי. That trope resembles a normal מֻנַּח but it appears with a vertical line (called פְּסִיק, *p'sik*) after the last letter of the word. This trope, called מֻנַּח לְגַרְמֵהּ (some call it simply לְגַרְמֵהּ, *l'garmeih*), looks like this:

It comes before מֻנַּח רְבִיעִי:

Sometimes you will see what appears to be מֻנַּח ׀ לְגַרְמֵהּ before other tropes, but it is considered מֻנַּח ׀ לְגַרְמֵהּ *only before* מֻנַּח רְבִיעִי. In those other instances, sing the trope as מֻנַּח, *not* מֻנַּח ׀ לְגַרְמֵהּ.

The following are examples of מֻנַּח ׀ לְגַרְמֵהּ:

מֻנַּח ׀
אוּלַי ׀
וְהָיָה ׀
לְבִשְׁעִי ׀

The last note of מֻנַּח ׀ לְגַרְמֵהּ is the same as the first note of מֻנַּח רְבִיעִי. Practice the following רְבִיעִי clauses, first with tropes, then with words:

17	רְבִיעִי ► מֻנַּח ► מֻנַּח ׀
18	רְבִיעִי ► מֻנַּח
19	רְבִיעִי

וְהָיָ֣ה ׀ שְׁאֵרִ֣ית יַעֲקֹ֗ב
אוּלַ֣י ׀ נִמְצָ֣א חָצִ֗יר
לְבֻשִׁ֣י ׀ בְּגְדֵ֣י תִפְאַרְתֶּ֗ךָ
כִּי־יָדְע֣וּ הָאֲנָשִׁ֗ים
בַּיּ֥וֹם הַה֖וּא

דַּרְגָּ֥א, which you learned in lesson 7, often precedes מֻנַּ֣ח רְבִיעִֽי. Here are some examples of דַּרְגָּ֥א leading to מֻנַּ֣ח רְבִיעִֽי. Chant the tropes first, then the words.

דַּרְגָּ֥א ◄ מֻנַּ֣ח רְבִיעִֽי
וְלֹ֣א יִטַּמְא֣וּ ע֗וֹד
וַתֹּ֣אמֶר ל֣וֹ אִשְׁתּ֗וֹ

To review all the tropes you have learned so far, chant the following phrases from haftarah. Remember to follow the four-step approach and break down the verses into the various clauses or trope families.

וְהָיָ֤ה יְהֹוָה֙ לְמֶ֣לֶךְ עַל־כָּל־הָאָ֔רֶץ
בַּיּ֣וֹם הַה֗וּא יִהְיֶ֧ה יְהֹוָ֛ה אֶחָ֖ד וּשְׁמ֥וֹ אֶחָֽד׃

And *Adonai* shall reign over all the earth; on that day *Adonai* shall be one, and known to be one. (Zechariah 14:9)

אָ֚ז תָּבֹ֣אנָה שְׁתַּ֣יִם נָשִׁ֥ים זֹנ֖וֹת אֶל־הַמֶּ֑לֶךְ וַתַּעֲמֹ֖דְנָה לְפָנָֽיו׃

Then came there two women, who were harlots, to the king, and stood before him. (1 Kings 3:16)

וְהָיָ֣ה ׀ שְׁאֵרִ֣ית יַעֲקֹ֗ב בְּקֶ֙רֶב֙ עַמִּ֣ים רַבִּ֔ים
כְּטַל֙ מֵאֵ֣ת יְהֹוָ֔ה כִּרְבִיבִ֖ים עֲלֵי־עֵ֑שֶׂב
אֲשֶׁ֤ר לֹא־יְקַוֶּה֙ לְאִ֔ישׁ וְלֹ֥א יְיַחֵ֖ל לִבְנֵ֥י אָדָֽם׃

And the remnant of Jacob shall be in the midst of many people like dew from *Adonai*, like

the showers upon the grass, that do not delay for man, nor wait for the sons of men.
(Micah 5:6)

וַיֹּאמֶר אַחְאָב אֶל־עֹבַדְיָהוּ לֵךְ בָּאָרֶץ אֶל־כָּל־מַעְיְנֵי הַמַּיִם
וְאֶל כָּל־הַנְּחָלִים אוּלַי ׀ נִמְצָא חָצִיר וּנְחַיֶּה סוּס וָפֶרֶד
וְלוֹא נַכְרִית מֵהַבְּהֵמָה:

And Ahab said to Obadiah, "Go to the land, to all the water springs, and to all the brooks;
perhaps we may find grass to keep the horses and mules alive, that we lose not all the
beasts." (1 Kings 18:5)

וַיִּירְאוּ הָאֲנָשִׁים יִרְאָה גְדוֹלָה וַיֹּאמְרוּ אֵלָיו מַה־זֹּאת עָשִׂיתָ
כִּי־יָדְעוּ הָאֲנָשִׁים כִּי־מִלִּפְנֵי יְהוָה הוּא בֹרֵחַ כִּי הִגִּיד לָהֶם:

Then the men were very afraid, and said to him, "Why have you done this? For the men
knew that he had fled from the presence of *Adonai,* because he had told them." (Jonah 1:10)

וַיֹּאמֶר אֲלֵיהֶם שָׂאוּנִי וַהֲטִילֻנִי אֶל־הַיָּם וְיִשְׁתֹּק הַיָּם מֵעֲלֵיכֶם
כִּי יוֹדֵעַ אָנִי כִּי בְשֶׁלִּי הַסַּעַר הַגָּדוֹל הַזֶּה עֲלֵיכֶם:

And he said to them, Take me up, and throw me into the sea; then the sea will calm down
for you; for I know it is because of me that this great tempest is upon you. (Jonah 1:12)

עוּרִי עוּרִי לִבְשִׁי עֻזֵּךְ צִיּוֹן לִבְשִׁי ׀ בִּגְדֵי תִפְאַרְתֵּךְ
יְרוּשָׁלַ͏ִם עִיר הַקֹּדֶשׁ כִּי לֹא יוֹסִיף יָבֹא־בָךְ עוֹד עָרֵל וְטָמֵא:

Awake, awake; put on your strength, O Zion; put on your beautiful garments, O Jerusalem,
the holy city; from now on there shall no more come to you the uncircumcised and the
unclean. (Isaiah 52:1)

The *R'vi-i* Clause · מַעֲרֶכֶת רְבִיעִי

Part Two

Several more tropes and combinations will round out our understanding of the רְבִיעִי clause. Thus far you have encountered the connector trope קַדְמָא in two basic combinations:

1. Before מַהְפַּךְ
2. Before מֵרְכָא תְּבִיר or דַּרְגָּא תְּבִיר

קַדְמָא also appears before a trope that looks like its mirror image:

When this "mirror" trope follows קַדְמָא, we call it אַזְלָא (*azla*). This combination is called קַדְמָא וְאַזְלָא (*kadma v'azla*) and sounds like this:

קַדְמָא ◄ וְאַזְלָא ♪15 **57**

Practice the following examples with קַדְמָא וְאַזְלָא. For each one, chant the tropes first, then the words.

קַדְמָא ◄ וְאַזְלָא

בָּרוּךְ אַתָּה

וַיָּמָן אֱלֹהִים

וַיִּרְשׁוּ הַנֶּגֶב

וַיִּקְרָא יְהוֹנָתָן

When the "mirror" trope appears by itself or is preceded by מֻנָּח (but without קַדְמָא), we call it גֵּרֵשׁ (*geresh*), and it sounds very different.

גֵּרֵשׁ ♪16 **58**

Both אַזְלָא and גֵּרֶשׁ are separators. גֵּרֶשׁ is often (but not always) found on words with three or fewer syllables. Chant the following examples:

גֵּרֶשׁ **58**

הֵ֜מָּה

וַיָּ֜קֶם

וַיֵּ֜שֶׁב

One final trope brings this section to a close. It is גֵּרְשַׁ֞יִם (*gershayim*). It looks like a double גֵּרֶשׁ and always appears above the first letter of the last syllable of a word:

It sounds like this:

גֵּרְשַׁ֞יִם 20♪ **59**

Practice the following words with גֵּרְשַׁ֞יִם:

גֵּרְשַׁ֞יִם

וְהָ֞יָה

גַּם־נָפַ֞ל

מֵעוֹלָ֞ם

וְלֹא־אָכַ֞ל

גֵּרְשַׁ֞יִם can be preceded by מֻנַּח:

מֻנַּח גֵּרְשַׁ֞יִם 21♪ **60**

כִּי מֵעוֹלָ֞ם

כִּי עַל־כָּל־גִּבְעָ֞ה

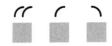

Practice the following trope combinations that can be part of the רְבִיעִי clause. If necessary, first chant the tropes separately, and then chant the words.

61

בָּרוּךְ אַתָּה יְיָ

וְהָיָה כְּעֵץ ׀ שָׁתוּל עַל־מַיִם

גַּם־נָפַל אִישׁ אֶל־רֵעֵהוּ

וְיָרְשׁוּ הַנֶּגֶב אֶת־הַר עֵשָׂו

וַיָּקֶם אֶת־הָעַמּוּד הַיְמָנִי

הֵמָּה יָבֹאוּ אֶל־מִקְדָּשִׁי

The following phrases from *N'vi-im* review most of the tropes you have learned so far. As usual, remember to first break down each verse into its clauses; next, chant the tropes; and then add the melodies to the words.

62

וְיָרְשׁוּ הַנֶּגֶב אֶת־הַר עֵשָׂו וְהַשְּׁפֵלָה אֶת־פְּלִשְׁתִּים

וְיָרְשׁוּ אֶת־שְׂדֵה אֶפְרַיִם וְאֵת שְׂדֵה שֹׁמְרוֹן

וּבִנְיָמִן אֶת־הַגִּלְעָד:

And they of the Negev shall possess the Mount of Esau; and they of the Sh'felah the land of the Philistines; and they shall possess the field of Ephraim, and the field of Samaria; and Benjamin shall possess Gilead. (Obadiah 1:19)

וְהָיָה כְּעֵץ ׀ שָׁתוּל עַל־מַיִם וְעַל־יוּבַל יְשַׁלַּח שָׁרָשָׁיו

וְלֹא יִרְאֶה כִּי־יָבֹא חֹם וְהָיָה עָלֵהוּ רַעֲנָן

וּבִשְׁנַת בַּצֹּרֶת לֹא יִדְאָג וְלֹא יָמִישׁ מֵעֲשׂוֹת פֶּרִי:

For he shall be like a tree planted by the waters, that spreads out its roots by the river, and shall not see when heat comes, but its leaf shall be green; and shall not be anxious in the year of drought, nor shall it cease from yielding fruit. (Jeremiah 17:8)

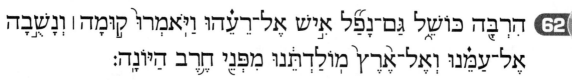

הִרְבָּה כּוֹשֵׁל גַּם־נָפַל אִישׁ אֶל־רֵעֵהוּ וַיֹּאמְרוּ קוּמָה ׀ וְנָשֻׁבָה
אֶל־עַמֵּנוּ וְאֶל־אֶרֶץ מוֹלַדְתֵּנוּ מִפְּנֵי חֶרֶב הַיּוֹנָה:

He made many to fall, indeed, one fell upon another; and they said, "Arise, and let us go again to our own people, and to the land of our birth, from the oppressing sword." (Jeremiah 46:16)

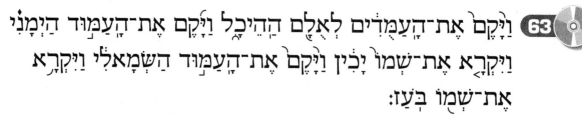

וַיָּקֶם אֶת־הָעַמֻּדִים לְאֻלָם הַהֵיכָל וַיָּקֶם אֶת־הָעַמּוּד הַיְמָנִי
וַיִּקְרָא אֶת־שְׁמוֹ יָכִין וַיָּקֶם אֶת־הָעַמּוּד הַשְּׂמָאלִי וַיִּקְרָא
אֶת־שְׁמוֹ בֹּעַז:

And he set up the pillars in the vestibule of the temple; and he set up the right pillar, and called its name Jachin; and he set up the left pillar, and called its name Boaz. (1 Kings 7:21)

הֵמָּה יָבֹאוּ אֶל־מִקְדָּשִׁי וְהֵמָּה יִקְרְבוּ אֶל־שֻׁלְחָנִי לְשָׁרְתֵנִי
וְשָׁמְרוּ אֶת־מִשְׁמַרְתִּי:

They shall enter into My sanctuary, and they shall come near to My table, to minister to Me, and they shall keep My charge. (Ezekiel 44:16)

וַיְהִי ׀ כִּזְרֹחַ הַשֶּׁמֶשׁ וַיְמַן אֱלֹהִים רוּחַ קָדִים חֲרִישִׁית וַתַּךְ
הַשֶּׁמֶשׁ עַל־רֹאשׁ יוֹנָה וַיִּתְעַלָּף וַיִּשְׁאַל אֶת־נַפְשׁוֹ לָמוּת
וַיֹּאמֶר טוֹב מוֹתִי מֵחַיָּי:

And it came to pass, when the sun rose, that God appointed a hot east wind; and the sun beat down upon the head of Jonah, so that he fainted, and wished to die, and said, "It is better for me to die than to live." (Jonah 4:8)

You have now learned all of the tropes that appear in the blessing before the reading of the haftarah. Try to chant it exactly according to the trope markings:

בָּרוּךְ אַתָּה יְיָ אֱלֹהֵינוּ מֶלֶךְ הָעוֹלָם, אֲשֶׁר בָּחַר בִּנְבִיאִים טוֹבִים, וְרָצָה בְדִבְרֵיהֶם הַנֶּאֱמָרִים בֶּאֱמֶת, בָּרוּךְ אַתָּה יְיָ, הַבּוֹחֵר בַּתּוֹרָה וּבְמֹשֶׁה עַבְדּוֹ, וּבְיִשְׂרָאֵל עַמּוֹ, וּבִנְבִיאֵי הָאֱמֶת וָצֶדֶק:

Blessed is *Adonai*, our God, Ruler of the universe, who has chosen faithful prophets to speak words of truth; blessed is *Adonai*, for the revelation of Torah, for Moses, God's servant and Israel God's people, and for the prophets of truth and righteousness.

For more practice, try the following section from *Haftarat Machar-Chodesh*, 1 Samuel 20:34–38.

וַיָּקָם יְהוֹנָתָן מֵעִם הַשֻּׁלְחָן בָּחֳרִי־אָף וְלֹא־אָכַל בְּיוֹם־הַחֹדֶשׁ הַשֵּׁנִי לֶחֶם כִּי נֶעְצַב אֶל־דָּוִד כִּי הִכְלִמוֹ אָבִיו: וַיְהִי בַבֹּקֶר וַיֵּצֵא יְהוֹנָתָן הַשָּׂדֶה לְמוֹעֵד דָּוִד וְנַעַר קָטֹן עִמּוֹ: וַיֹּאמֶר לְנַעֲרוֹ רֻץ מְצָא נָא אֶת־הַחִצִּים אֲשֶׁר אָנֹכִי מוֹרֶה הַנַּעַר רָץ וְהוּא־יָרָה הַחֵצִי לְהַעֲבִרוֹ: וַיָּבֹא הַנַּעַר עַד־מְקוֹם הַחֵצִי אֲשֶׁר יָרָה יְהוֹנָתָן וַיִּקְרָא יְהוֹנָתָן אַחֲרֵי הַנַּעַר וַיֹּאמֶר הֲלוֹא הַחֵצִי מִמְּךָ וָהָלְאָה: וַיִּקְרָא יְהוֹנָתָן אַחֲרֵי הַנַּעַר מְהֵרָה חוּשָׁה אַל־תַּעֲמֹד וַיְלַקֵּט נַעַר יְהוֹנָתָן אֶת־הַחִצִּים וַיָּבֹא אֶל־אֲדֹנָיו:

So Jonathan arose from the table in fierce anger, and ate no food on the second day of the new moon; for he was grieved for David, because his father had put him to shame. And it came to pass in the morning, that Jonathan went out to the field at the time appointed with David, and a little lad with him. And he said to his lad, "Run, find out now the arrows which I shoot." And as the lad ran, he shot an arrow beyond him. And when the lad came to the place of the arrow that Jonathan had shot, Jonathan cried after the lad, and said, "Is not the arrow beyond you?" And Jonathan cried after the lad, "Make speed, hurry, stay not," and Jonathan's lad gathered up the arrows, and came to his master. (1 Samuel 20:34–38)

T'lisha K'tanah • תְּלִישָׁא קְטַנָּה

Pazer • פָּזֵר

T'lisha G'dolah • תְּלִישָׁא גְדוֹלָה

Before you learn the sixth and last trope clause, it is important to discuss three tropes that appear frequently in a variety of clauses and combinations. The first, תְּלִישָׁא קְטַנָּה (t'lisha-k'tanah), is notated above a word and looks like a circle with a small tail jutting out on its right, like this:

Like פַּשְׁטָא, תְּלִישָׁא קְטַנָּה is postpositive; that is, it always appears *above the last letter of a word*. And just as with פַּשְׁטָא, if the word is accented somewhere other than on the final syllable, the trope will appear a second time over the accented syllable.

תְּלִישָׁא קְטַנָּה is a מְחַבֵּר and can be found in the *r'vi-i* clause, the *t'vir* clause, the *katon* clause, and the *segol* clause, which will be taught in the next lesson—in other words, in every clause except the *etnachta* and *sof-pasuk* clauses. The notes are close together, going up, down, up, up, and back down to the original note in thirds, like this:

תְּלִישָׁא קְטַנָּה **66**

Practice the following words with תְּלִישָׁא קְטַנָּה:

תְּלִישָׁא קְטַנָּה
כָּל־חֻקֹּתָיו
וַיְהִי
וַיָּשֶׂם
וַתָּקָם

תְּלִישָׁא קְטַנָּה is often served by מֻנַּח. This מֻנַּח jumps up and then flows right into תְּלִישָׁא קְטַנָּה. Listen:

מֻנַּח תְּלִישָׁא קְטַנָּה 30

Chant the following combinations of מֻנַּח תְּלִישָׁא קְטַנָּה:

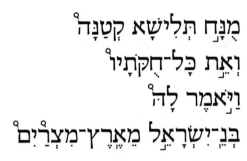

מֻנַּח תְּלִישָׁא קְטַנָּה

וְאֵת כָּל־חֻקֹּתָיו

וַיֹּאמֶר לָהֶ

בְּנֵי־יִשְׂרָאֵל מֵאֶרֶץ־מִצְרַיִם

פָּזֵר (*pazer*) is the next trope you will learn in this lesson. It is a מַפְסִיק and can appear in almost every clause except *sof-pasuk*. It looks like an upside-down chair:

פ

Its melody rises and then descends and then circles around the ending note, like this:

פָּזֵר 68

Chant the following words with פָּזֵר:

הַמֶּלֶךְ

יֵשֶׁב־בָּהּ

וּשְׁמוֹ

יָדַעְתָּ

פָּזֵר is often served by the same מֻנַּח you learned before תְּלִישָׁא קְטַנָּה.

68 31♪ מֻנַּח פָּזֵר

וַיְצַו הַמֶּלֶךְ

אֲשֶׁר יֶשׁ־בָּהּ

אַתָּה יָדַעְתָּ

תְּלִישָׁא גְדוֹלָה (t'lisha-g'dolah), the last trope in this lesson, is often confused with תְּלִישָׁא קְטַנָּה.

Despite their similarity in name and appearance, the two are quite different in function. Here are some ways to tell them apart:

- The little tail on תְּלִישָׁא גְדוֹלָה points to the left: (sign leans to the right)
- תְּלִישָׁא גְדוֹלָה is a מַפְסִיק, whereas תְּלִישָׁא קְטַנָּה is a מְחַבֵּר.
- תְּלִישָׁא גְדוֹלָה *always appears over the first letter of a word;* it is thus called a *prepositive* trope. If the accent falls on a syllable other than the first, you will see a second , indicating the accented syllable.

תְּלִישָׁא גְדוֹלָה sounds like a four-note scale that goes up and then returns to the same note on which it began:

69 תְּלִישָׁא גְדוֹלָה

Chant the following words with תְּלִישָׁא גְדוֹלָה:

תְּלִישָׁא גְדוֹלָה

בְּנֵי־הַנְּבִיאִים

אֶלְקָנָה

הַמֶּלֶךְ

יִשְׂרָאֵל

תְּלִישָׁא גְדוֹלָה is also often preceded by מֵנָח. When מֵנָח precedes any of the three tropes presented in this chapter, it has the same melody each time:

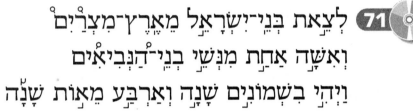

מֵנָח תְּלִישָׁא גְדוֹלָה
וַיֵּשֶׁב הַמֶּלֶךְ
מֵנַשֵּׁי בְּנֵי־הַנְּבִיאִֽים
צוּרַת הַבַּיִת
בְּנֵי־יִשְׂרָאֵל מֵאֶרֶץ־מִצְרַיִם

Sometimes more than one מֵנָח may precede תְּלִישָׁא קְטַנָה, פָּזֵר, or תְּלִישָׁא גְדוֹלָה. In that case, you repeat the melody for מֵנָח each time, as in the following examples:

לְצֵאת בְּנֵי־יִשְׂרָאֵל מֵאֶרֶץ־מִצְרַיִם
וְאִשָּׁה אַחַת מִנְשֵׁי בְּנֵי־הַנְּבִיאִֽים
וַיְהִי בִשְׁמוֹנִים שָׁנָה וְאַרְבַּע מֵאוֹת שָׁנָֽה

You are now ready to chant some more complex combinations that include תְּלִישָׁא קְטַנָה, פָּזֵר, and תְּלִישָׁא גְדוֹלָה.

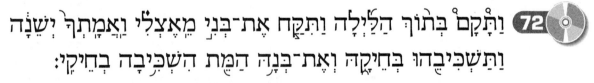

וַתָּקָם בְּתוֹךְ הַלַּיְלָה וַתִּקַּח אֶת־בְּנִי מֵאֶצְלִי וַאֲמָתְךָ יְשֵׁנָה
וַתַּשְׁכִּיבֵהוּ בְחֵיקָהּ וְאֶת־בְּנָהּ הַמֵּת הִשְׁכִּיבָה בְחֵיקִֽי:

And she arose at midnight, and took my son from my side, while your maidservant slept, and laid it in her bosom, and laid her dead child in my bosom. (1 Kings 3:20)

וְאִשָּׁה אַחַת מִנְשֵׁי בְנֵי־הַנְּבִיאִים צָעֲקָה אֶל־אֱלִישָׁע לֵאמֹר
עַבְדְּךָ אִישִׁי מֵת וְאַתָּה יָדַעְתָּ כִּי עַבְדְּךָ הָיָה יָרֵא אֶת־יְהֹוָה
וְהַנֹּשֶׁה בָּא לָקַחַת אֶת־שְׁנֵי יְלָדַי לוֹ לַעֲבָדִֽים:

The wife of one of the prophetic disciples cried out to Elisha, saying: "Your servant my husband has died. You know how your servant always revered the Eternal. Now a creditor is coming to take away my two sons to be his slaves." (2 Kings 4:1)

וַיְהִי אִישׁ אֶחָד מִן־הָרָמָתַיִם צוֹפִים מֵהַר אֶפְרָיִם
וּשְׁמוֹ אֶלְקָנָה בֶּן־יְרֹחָם בֶּן־אֱלִיהוּא בֶּן־תֹּחוּ בֶן־צוּף אֶפְרָתִי:

And there was a certain man of Ramathaim-Zophim, of Mount Ephraim, and his name was Elkanah, the son of Jeroham, the son of Elihu, the son of Tohu, the son of Zuph, an Ephrathite. (1 Samuel 1:1)

וַיֹּאמֶר לָהּ אֶלְקָנָה אִישָׁהּ עֲשִׂי הַטּוֹב בְּעֵינַיִךְ שְׁבִי עַד־גׇּמְלֵךְ
אֹתוֹ אַךְ יָקֵם יְהֹוָה אֶת־דְּבָרוֹ וַתֵּשֶׁב הָאִשָּׁה וַתֵּינֶק אֶת־בְּנָהּ
עַד־גׇּמְלָהּ אֹתוֹ:

Elkanah, her husband, said to her: "Do what seems good to you; stay until you've weaned him; only may the Eternal fulfill the Divine promise." So the woman remained and nursed her son until she had weaned him. (1 Samuel 1:23)

וַיְצַו הַמֶּלֶךְ וַיַּסִּעוּ אֲבָנִים גְּדֹלוֹת אֲבָנִים יְקָרוֹת לְיַסֵּד הַבָּיִת
אַבְנֵי גָזִית:

And the king commanded, and they brought great stones, costly stones, to lay the foundation of the house with dressed stones. (1 Kings 5:31)

וַאֲנִי לֹא אָחוּס עַל־נִינְוֵה הָעִיר הַגְּדוֹלָה
אֲשֶׁר יֶשׁ־בָּהּ הַרְבֵּה מִשְׁתֵּים־עֶשְׂרֵה רִבּוֹ אָדָם
אֲשֶׁר לֹא־יָדַע בֵּין־יְמִינוֹ לִשְׂמֹאלוֹ וּבְהֵמָה רַבָּה:

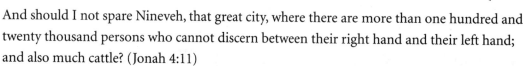

And should I not spare Nineveh, that great city, where there are more than one hundred and twenty thousand persons who cannot discern between their right hand and their left hand; and also much cattle? (Jonah 4:11)

וַיֵּשֶׁב הַמֶּלֶךְ עַל־מוֹשָׁבוֹ כְּפַעַם ׀ בְּפַעַם אֶל־מוֹשַׁב הַקִּיר
וַיָּקׇם יְהוֹנָתָן וַיֵּשֶׁב אַבְנֵר מִצַּד שָׁאוּל וַיִּפָּקֵד מְקוֹם דָּוִד:

And the king sat upon his seat, as at other times, upon a seat by the wall; and Jonathan arose, and Abner sat by Saul's side, and David's place was empty. (1 Samuel 20:25)

וְאִם־נִכְלְמ֞וּ מִכֹּ֣ל אֲשֶׁר־עָשׂ֗וּ צוּרַ֣ת הַבַּ֡יִת וּתְכוּנָת֣וֹ וּמוֹצָאָ֣יו
וּמ֣וֹבָאָ֣יו וְכָל־צוּרֹתָ֡יו וְאֵ֣ת כָּל־חֻקֹּתָיו֩ וְכָל־צ֨וּרֹתָ֤יו וְכָל־תּֽוֹרֹתָיו֙
הוֹדַ֣ע אוֹתָ֔ם וּכְתֹ֖ב לְעֵֽינֵיהֶ֑ם וְיִשְׁמְר֞וּ אֶת־כָּל־צוּרָת֗וֹ וְאֶת־כָּל־
חֻקֹּתָ֛יו וְעָשׂ֥וּ אוֹתָֽם׃

And if they are ashamed of all that they have done, describe to them the form of the House,
and its fashion, and its exits, and its entrances, and all its forms, and all its ordinances, and
all its shapes, and all its laws; and write it in their sight, that they may keep its whole form,
and all its ordinances, and do them. (Ezekiel 43:11)

The *Segol* Clause • מַעֲרֶכֶת סֶגּוֹל

So far you have learned five major families of tropes or trope clauses. You have seen that each of these clauses is governed by (and named after) the "head" trope with which the clause concludes. The clauses you have learned thus far are:

1. מַעֲרֶכֶת אֶתְנַחְתָּא   (*etnachta* clause)

2. מַעֲרֶכֶת סוֹף־פָּסוּק: (*sof-pasuk* clause)

3. מַעֲרֶכֶת קָטֹן   (*katon* clause)

4. מַעֲרֶכֶת תְּבִיר   (*t'vir* clause)

5. מַעֲרֶכֶת רְבִיעִי   (*r'vi-i* clause)

Each of the separator tropes is served by connector tropes. Although the vast majority of these connector tropes are found within many clauses, some are found only within a certain clause. For example:

מֻנַּח is found in all of the clauses (albeit with varying melodies).

דַּרְגָּא is found in the רְבִיעִי and תְּבִיר clauses only, not in any others.

מַהְפָּךְ is found only in the קָטֹן clause.

In Appendix B, you will find a detailed chart of most of the possibilities within the clauses.

In this lesson you will learn the sixth and final trope clause, known as סֶגּוֹל (*segol*). סֶגּוֹל is the Hebrew word for "cluster," as in a cluster of grapes. The trope indeed looks like a cluster:

It sounds like this:

סֶגּוֹל

סֶגּוֹל is a מַפְסִיק and is preceded, although not always immediately, by זַרְקָא (*zarka*), a מְחַבֵּר. The symbol for זַרְקָא looks like this:

And the trope sounds like this:

זַרְקָא

Both זַרְקָא and סֶגּוֹל are postpositive tropes. Just like תְּלִישָׁא־קְטַנָּה and פַּשְׁטָא, they always appear *above the final letter of a word.*

If a word is accented somewhere other than on the final syllable, the trope symbol will appear a second time over the accented syllable. You are now ready to learn the chanting of this combination.

First chant זַרְקָא סֶגּוֹל:

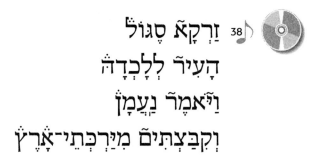

זַרְקָא סֶגּוֹל
הָעִיר לְלָכְדָהּ
וַיֹּאמֶר נַעֲמָן
וְקִבַּצְתִּים מִיַּרְכְּתֵי־אָרֶץ

When מֻנַּח precedes זַרְקָא֮, its melody leads right into זַרְקָא֮:

זַרְקָא֮ סֶגּוֹל֒ ← מֻנַּח ♪36 **75** ◎

נְשֵׁיכֶם טַפְּכֶם֒ וּמִקְנֵיכֶ֫ם

כִּי־יַגִּיעַ גֵּי־הָרִים֒ אֶל־אָצַל֒

כִּי־נִכְמְר֫וּ רַחֲמָיו֮ עַל־בְּנ֫וֹ

מֻנַּח before סֶגּוֹל֒ is a natural musical connector:

זַרְקָא֮ ← מֻנַּח ← סֶגּוֹל֒ ♪37 **76** ◎

יִתָּקַ֫ע בְּשׁוֹפָ֫ר גָּדוֹל֒

וַיָּק֫וּמוּ וַיָּנֻ֫סוּ בַּנֶּ֫שֶׁף֒

וַיִּזְעֲק֫וּ אִישׁ אֶל־אֱלֹהָיו֒

מֻנַּח ← זַרְקָא֮ ← מֻנַּח ← סֶגּוֹל֒ ♪35 **77** ◎

וַתֵּצֵא יָעֵל֒ לִקְרַאת סִיסְרָא֮

וּדְמוּת פְּנֵיהֶם֒ פְּנֵי אָדָ֫ם

מֶ֫לֶךְ בְּנֵי־עַמּוֹן֒ בָּא עֲלֵיכֶ֫ם

Here are some verses from *N'vi-im* that include the סֶגּוֹל clause. As the examples get longer, remember to break each verse down into its major clauses. Then practice each clause separately before you attempt to chant the entire verse.

הִנֵּה הַסֹּלְלוֹת בָּאוּ הָעִיר לְלָכְדָהּ וְהָעִיר נִתְּנָה בְּיַד הַכַּשְׂדִּים
הַנִּלְחָמִים עָלֶיהָ מִפְּנֵי הַחֶרֶב וְהָרָעָב וְהַדָּבֶר וַאֲשֶׁר דִּבַּרְתָּ
הָיָה וְהִנְּךָ רֹאֶה:

Behold the siege works, they have come to the city to take it; and the city is given to the hand of the Chaldeans, who fight against it, because of the sword, and of the famine, and of the pestilence; and what You have spoken has come to pass; and, behold, You see it.
(Jeremiah 32:24)

הִנְנִי מֵבִיא אוֹתָם מֵאֶרֶץ צָפוֹן וְקִבַּצְתִּים מִיַּרְכְּתֵי־אָרֶץ
בָּם עִוֵּר וּפִסֵּחַ הָרָה וְיֹלֶדֶת יַחְדָּו קָהָל גָּדוֹל יָשׁוּבוּ הֵנָּה:

Behold, I will bring them from the north country, and gather them from the ends of the earth, and with them the blind and the lame, the woman with child and she who labors with child together; a great company shall return there. (Jeremiah 31:8)

וַיִּירְאוּ הַמַּלָּחִים וַיִּזְעֲקוּ אִישׁ אֶל־אֱלֹהָיו וַיָּטִלוּ אֶת־הַכֵּלִים
אֲשֶׁר בָּאֳנִיָּה אֶל־הַיָּם לְהָקֵל מֵעֲלֵיהֶם
וְיוֹנָה יָרַד אֶל־יַרְכְּתֵי הַסְּפִינָה וַיִּשְׁכַּב וַיֵּרָדַם:

Then the sailors were afraid, and cried each one to his own god, and they threw the wares that were in the ship to the sea, to lighten it for them. But Jonah had gone down into the interior of the ship; and had lain down, and was fast asleep. (Jonah 1:5)

וַתֵּצֵא יָעֵל לִקְרַאת סִיסְרָא וַתֹּאמֶר אֵלָיו סוּרָה אֲדֹנִי סוּרָה
אֵלַי אַל־תִּירָא וַיָּסַר אֵלֶיהָ הָאֹהֱלָה וַתְּכַסֵּהוּ בַּשְּׂמִיכָה:

And Yael went out to meet Sisera, and said to him, "Turn in, my lord, turn in to me; fear not." And when he had turned in to her into the tent, she covered him with a mantle.
(Judges 4:18)

You Can Chant Haftarah!

As you begin to prepare haftarah portions, you will no doubt find that there is a vast amount of material to cover. In this chapter we offer some guidelines that have been found useful for approaching a haftarah reading in the most effective way.

We'll look first at Jonah 4:10 because this verse presents some typical and interesting trope combinations for us to study.

וַיֹּ֣אמֶר יְהוָ֗ה אַתָּ֤ה חַ֙סְתָּ֙ עַל־הַקִּ֣יקָי֔וֹן אֲשֶׁ֥ר לֹא־עָמַ֖לְתָּ בּ֑וֹ
וְלֹ֣א גִדַּלְתּ֔וֹ שֶׁבִּן־לַ֥יְלָה הָיָ֖ה וּבִן־לַ֥יְלָה אָבָֽד׃

Then *Adonai* said, "You had concern for the plant, for which you did not labor, nor did you make it grow; which came up in a night, and perished in a night." (Jonah 4:10)

1. Be sure that you read the Hebrew text correctly. Did you see the penultimate accent on the word וַיֹּ֣אמֶר? Were you sure to say חַ֙סְתָּ֙, with the accent on the first syllable, **chas**-ta?

2. It's a good idea to look through the verse, separating the trope clauses so that you have an idea of its overall structure. In this particular verse you should have counted five clauses:

   • A *katon* clause ending with the word יְהוָ֗ה
   • Another *katon* clause ending with the words עַל־הַקִּ֣יקָי֔וֹן
   • A *t'vir* clause on the single word אֲשֶׁ֥ר
   • An *etnachta* clause ending with the word גִדַּלְתּ֔וֹ
   • The *sof-pasuk* clause ending the verse with the word אָבָֽד׃

3. Chant the tropes carefully—if necessary, clause by clause.
   • Notice the unusual combination of מֵרְכָ֥א followed by פַּשְׁטָא֙. The מֵרְכָ֥א is chanted as the first note of the פַּשְׁטָא֙.

4. Chant the words.

If you're hungry for more examples, turn to 1 Samuel 2:5 and meet some other people who are hungry.

שְׂבֵעִים בַּלֶּחֶם נִשְׂכָּרוּ וּרְעֵבִים חָדֵלּוּ
עַד־עֲקָרָה יָלְדָה שִׁבְעָה וְרַבַּת בָּנִים אֻמְלָלָה:

Those who were full have hired out themselves for bread; and those who were hungry ceased to hunger; the barren has borne seven; and she who has many children has become wretched. (1 Samuel 2:5)

1. Read the words. That first word is שְׂבֵעִים—*s'vei'im*, not *sh'vei'im*. בַּלֶּחֶם is stressed on the second syllable.

2. Analyze the clauses.
   - The *katon* clause ends on the third word of the verse, נִשְׂכָּרוּ.
   - The *etnachta* clause ends two words later with חָדֵלּוּ.
   - The *katon* clause ends three words later with שִׁבְעָה.
   - The verse concludes with אֻמְלָלָה:.

3. Chant the tropes.

4. Chant the words.

Now, let's try one more example, Isaiah 40:10:

הִנֵּה אֲדֹנָי יֱהֹוִה בְּחָזָק יָבוֹא וּזְרֹעוֹ מֹשְׁלָה לוֹ הִנֵּה שְׂכָרוֹ
אִתּוֹ וּפְעֻלָּתוֹ לְפָנָיו:

Behold the Eternal God coming in might, coming to rule with [outstretched] arm, bringing [divine] reward and recompense [from on high]. (Isaiah 40:10)

1. Read the words. Did you notice that the vowels on the third word are a little unusual? You would expect to see יְהֹוָה, which would be pronounced *Adonai*. However in this verse, the word אֲדֹנָי is spelled out. When that happens, it is frequently followed by יֱהֹוִה, which contains the same vowels as the word אֱלֹהִים, another name for God, and is indeed pronounced as *Elohim*.

You should also notice the penultimate accent on the word מֹשְׁלָה. Sing the trope melody on the first syllable, *mosh-*, and then add one last note on the last syllable, *-lah*.

2. Analyze the clauses.
   - The *katon* clause ends on the fifth word of the verse, יָבוֹא.
   - The *etnachta* clause ends three words later with לוֹ.
   - The *katon* clause ends three words later with אֹתוֹ.
   - The verse concludes with לְפָנָיו:.

3. Chant the tropes. Make sure you chant the first trope as קַדְמָא. You can clearly see that it is *not* over the last letter and that it is followed by מַהְפַּךְ. The rest of the tropes are straightforward.

"Cantillation": A Historical Overview

From the *Encyclopedia of Judaism*, Eliyahu Schleifer, Jerusalem, 1989[6]

Cantillation The art of the liturgical chanting of the Bible. Jewish liturgical regulations require that various portions of the Bible be read ceremoniously in public services. Portions of the Pentateuch are read during the morning services on Mondays, Thursdays, Saturdays, New Moons, Festivals, and the High Holidays. A portion from the Prophets is read on Saturdays, Festivals, and Holidays (this portion is called the "haftarah"). Other books are read on appropriate occasions: the Scrolls of Song of Songs, Ruth, and Ecclesiastes on the Three Pilgrim Festivals; the Scroll of Esther on Purim; and Lamentations on the Ninth of Av (Tishah B'Av).

The public reading of the Pentateuch and the Scrolls is usually executed by a professional or semiprofessional reader called a *ba-al k'riyah* or *ba-al koreh* (in the Yemenite tradition the Pentateuch is read by laymen), and with the exception of some Reform synagogues, the reading is always chanted. The art of chanting is ancient and may date back to Second Temple times, but the different melodic patterns used by the various Jewish communities developed much later, perhaps during the Middle Ages, and have continued to grow and change ever since.

The cantillation of Scripture is expected to adhere to the signs called *t'amim* or *ta-amei hamikra*. These were developed together with the punctuation signs in Babylonia and Eretz Yisrael during the talmudic and post-talmudic periods; they were first transmitted orally and were later codified in various notation systems, the fullest and most important of which was the one developed by the Masoretic school of Tiberias in the ninth and tenth centuries C.E. The Tiberian sages assigned three functions to the accents (*t'amim*): (a) to show the proper accentuation of the words; (b) to divide the biblical verses properly and thus help preserve the acceptable interpretation of the text; and (c) to indicate the melodic patterns that should be used with each part of the verse. Because of this last function, the signs are also called *n'ginot* (melodies). The codices compiled by these scholars (the most famous of which are the Crown of Aleppo, c. 920 C.E., now in Jerusalem, and the Leningrad Codex, c.1010) have been accepted as the authorized versions of the Hebrew Bible.

The signs of the accents are marked only in the Masoretic codices and in the printed Bibles. They are never copied in the scrolls that are used for the liturgical reading in the synagogue. In most communities it is customary to read the portion of the Prophets from a codex or a

---

6 Reprinted with permission from the author.

printed Bible, but the Pentateuch and the Five Scrolls are read from scrolls. In the latter cases, the reader is obliged to memorize the signs in order to effect a correct cantillation. As a practicing device, modern readers use a book called *tikkun lakorim,* which contains the original text as written in the scroll side-by-side with the Masoretic version, which includes the punctuation and accents, in two parallel columns. An earlier means of overcoming the lack of accents in the scrolls was the use of a prompter (*somech*), who indicated the accents to the reader by a system of hand signals called cheironomy. Some of the accents may have derived their names from the cheironomical signals that accompany them. Cheironomy is still in use in some Jewish communities, with some preserving the old customs and others inventing new methods.

The Masoretic accents of Tiberias are organized into two graphical systems: one for the Psalms, Proverbs, and the central part of Job and a second system for the other twenty-one books of the Bible. Only the latter is relevant to the ceremonial reading of Scripture in public. The system contains twenty-eight signs, most of which are written above and some below the letters, and one sign follows the relevant word. The signs are classified as (a) Disjunctives or Lords, which mark the end of verses and divide the latter into phrases, clauses, and subclauses; and (b) Conjunctives, or Servants, whose task is to link the words within the division or subdivision of a verse. The Disjunctives are hierarchical, based on the degree of closure that they affect. Their placement in the text was determined by syntactical, exegetical, and musical considerations.

The signs of the *t'amim* are universally accepted by all Jews. However, their musical interpretation differs from one community to the next. One can speak of eight main musical traditions of cantillation:

1. Southern Arab Peninsula: Yemen and Hadramaut. This is perhaps one of the oldest traditions of cantillation. Theoretically it recognizes all the signs of the *t'amim*, but in practice, some are not used. The style of chanting may suggest that the tradition is based on an earlier system of cantillation, such as was recorded in the Babylonian notation during the seventh century and earlier.

2. The Middle East: Iran, Bukhara, Kurdistan, Georgia, and the northern parts of Iraq. Another old tradition, perhaps based partially on the old Babylonian system of notation but musically different from the Yemenite tradition.

3. The Near East: Turkey, Syria, central Iraq, Lebanon, and Egypt. This is known as the Eastern Sephardic Tradition. It can be heard in some Greek and Balkan communities

and has become the dominant style of the non-Ashkenazi communities of Israel. The readers of the Pentateuch strive to give musical meaning to each sign, but some of the signs are ignored in the reading of the Prophets and other books. The musical motives are influenced by the Arabic modes of the *maqam*.

4. North Africa: Libya, Tunisia, Algeria, and Morocco. This tradition reflects the influence of African pentatonic patterns, especially in communities far from the shores of the Mediterranean.

5. Italy. The ancient tradition of the Italian Jews can still be heard in Rome and the Roman Jewish community of Jerusalem. Cheironomy is still used by some of those readers.

6. The Sephardic and Portuguese communities of Europe. The so-called Western Sephardim may preserve the main features of the original Sephardic cantillation melodies.

7. Western European Ashkenazim: German-speaking countries, France, some communities of the Netherlands, and England. This tradition, which developed in medieval times, was first recorded in European cantorial manuals of the nineteenth century.

8. East-European Ashkenazim. This tradition developed out of the Western Ashkenazi cantillation and has become the dominant style among the Ashkenazi communities of Israel and English-speaking countries. The Lithuanian version of this tradition is perhaps the most meticulous musical system in existence.

Most of the eight musical traditions have diverse subtraditions. Considerable musical differences exist among the various countries within one tradition and even different parts of the same country. In addition, each tradition has different melodic patterns for various divisions of the Bible or for different liturgical occasions. Thus, for example, the East-European Ashkenazi tradition consists of six musical systems: the regular Pentateuch reading; the High Holiday version of the same; the Prophets; the Book of Esther; the Song of Songs, Ruth, and Ecclesiastes; and Lamentations.

We have spoken of the tropes either as מַפְסִיקִים, separators, or מְחַבְּרִים. The מַפְסִיקִים may bring a phrase to a temporary pause — like טִפְחָא—or to an undeniably final cadence—like סוֹף־פָּסוּק. The מְחַבְּרִים—like מֵרְכָא and מַהְפָּךְ—bind words together and ensure an uninterrupted flow within a phrase.

An analysis of 1 Samuel 1:10 illustrates the contrasting functions of מְחַבְּרִים and מַפְסִיקִים. The function of each trope is notated beneath the symbol.

וְהִיא ◄ מָרַת ◄ נֶפֶשׁ ◄ וַתִּתְפַּלֵּל ◄ עַל־יְהֹוָה ◄ וּבָכֹה ◄ תִבְכֶּה:

(mafsik | m'chaber ◄ mafsik | m'chaber ◄ mafsik | m'chaber ◄ mafsik ||)

separator   connector   separator   connector   separator   connector   separator

The English translation demonstrates the elegant manner in which the tropes fulfill their most important function—revealing the meaning of the sacred text:

And she (Hannah)…was in bitterness of soul……and prayed to *Adonai*… and wept bitterly.

You may have noticed that the space or pause after "And she" is half as long as the space or pause after "soul." This is due to the fact that while אֶתְנַחְתָּא and טִפְחָא are both מַפְסִיקִים, אֶתְנַחְתָּא is the stronger one. It is considered an "emperor," while טִפְחָא is considered a "king," one rung lower in the cantillation hierarchy. When you chant this verse, you will want to pause considerably after סוֹף־פָּסוּק, clearly pause after אֶתְנַחְתָּא, and pause slightly after טִפְחָא. If you do this, the meaning of the words will become clear.

On the following pages you will find two different tables. The first one lists each of the טַעֲמֵי הַמִקְרָא, together with its symbol, name, and meaning. First the מַפְסִיקִים are prsented in hierarchical order and then the מְחַבְּרִים.

The second table shows all of the trope clauses or families, listing all the tropes you may find in each clause and nearly all the relationships among them.

TROPE TABLE A

	"Hierarchy"	Symbol	Name	Meaning
MAFSIKIM (Separators)	**"Emperors"** (long pause)		סוֹף־פָּסוּק *sof-pasuk*	end of sentence
			אֶתְנַחְתָּא *etnachta*	to rest
	"Kings" (shorter pause than "Emperors")		סֶגוֹל *segol*	cluster
			שַׁלְשֶׁלֶת *shalshelet*	chain
			(זָקֵף) קָטֹן (*zakef*) *katon*	lesser upright
			זָקֵף גָּדוֹל *zakef gadol*	full upright
			רְבִיעִי *r'vi-i*	four-square
	"Dukes" Shorter pause than "Kings")		טִפְחָא *tipcha*	handbreath
			פַּשְׁטָא *pashta*	extending
			יְתִיב *y'tiv*	staying
			זַרְקָא *zarka*	scattered
			מֻנָּח ׀ לְגַרְמֵהּ *munach l'garmeih*	independent *munach*
	"Officers" (shorter pause than "Dukes")		תְּבִיר *t'vir*	broken
			גֵּרֵשׁ *geresh*	to chase
			אַזְלָא *azla*	going on
			גֵּרְשַׁיִם *gershayim*	double *geresh*
			פָּזֵר *pazer*	to scatter
			תְּלִישָׁא גְדוֹלָה *t'lisha g'dolah*	big *t'lisha*
			קַרְנֵי פָרָה *karnei parah*	horns of a heifer
M'CHABRIM (Conectors)			מֵרְכָא *mercha*	to lengthen
			מֻנָּח *munach*	sustained
			מַהְפָּךְ *mapach*	reversed
			קַדְמָא *kadma*	to proceed
			דַּרְגָּא *darga*	stepwise
			תְּלִישָׁא קְטַנָּה *t'lisha k'tanah*	small *t'lisha*
			יֵרַח בֶּן יוֹמוֹ *yare-ach ben yomo*	moon of one day
			מֵרְכָא כְּפוּלָה *mercha k'fulah*	double *mercha*

TROPE TABLE B

I. *Sof-Pasuk* Clause

Name	Symbol	Function	Serves	Served by
sof-pasuk		mafsik		tipcha mercha
tipcha		mafsik	sof-pasuk	mercha
mercha		m'chaber	sof-pasuk tipcha	

II. *Etnachta* Clause

Name	Symbol	Function	Serves	Served by
etnachta		mafsik		tipcha munach
tipcha		mafsik	etnachta	mercha
munach		m'chaber	etnachta	
mercha		m'chaber	tipcha	

III. *Katon* Clause

Name	Symbol	Function	Serves	Served by
katon		mafsik		munach pashta y'tiv
pashta		mafsik	katon	mapach mercha
munach		m'chaber	katon mapach	
mapach		m'chaber	pashta	munach
kadma		m'chaber	mapach	
zakef gadol		mafsik		
y'tiv		mafsik	munach katon	
t'lisha g'dolah		mafsik		munach

IV. *T'vir* Clause

Name	Symbol	Function	Serves	Served by
t'vir	׳	mafsik		darga mercha
darga	֧	m'chaber	t'vir	munach kadma
mercha	֜	m'chaber	t'vir	munach kadma
mercha k'fulah	֦	m'chaber		darga
munach	ֻ	m'chaber	darga mercha t'lisha k'tanah	
kadma	֤	m'chaber	darga mercha	
t'lisha k'tanah	֠	m'chaber	kadma	munach
gershayim	֞	mafsik		munach

V. *R'vi-i* Clause

Name	Symbol	Function	Serves	Served by
r'vi-i	֗	mafsik		munach kadma v'azla gershayim
munach l'garmeih	׀	mafsik	munach r'vi-i	darga kadma v'azla geresh
azla	֝	mafsik		kadma
munach	ֻ	m'chaber	r'vi-i	munach l'garmeih darga kadma v'azla geresh gershayim
kadma	֤	m'chaber	azla	t'lisha k'tanah
gershayim	֞	mafsik		munach

V. *R'vi-i* Clause (continued)

Name	Symbol	Function	Serves	Served by
geresh		mafsik		munach kadma t'lisha g'dolah
darga		m'chaber	munach r'vi-i	munach kadma
pazer		mafsik		munach
t'lisha k'tanah		m'chaber	kadma	munach
yare-ach ben yomo		m'chaber	karnei parah	munach
karnei parah		mafsik		yare-ach ben yomo

VI. *Segol* Clause

Name	Symbol	Function	Serves	Served by
segol		mafsik		zarka munach
zarka		m'chaber	segol	munach
munach		m'chaber	segol zarka	
shalshelet		mafsik		
mercha		m'chaber	zarka	
kadma		m'chaber	munach mercha	

Parashiyot and Haftarot–Torah and Haftarah Portions

Many customs surround the readings from *Tanach*. The Torah is divided into fifty-four weekly portions called פָּרָשִׁיּוֹת (*parashiyot*) or סְדָרוֹת (*sidrot*). The title of each פָּרָשָׁה (*parashah*, singular) is usually, but not always, based upon its first important word. The third פָּרָשָׁה in the Book of Genesis, for example, is called *Lech L'cha*. The final פָּרָשָׁה in Deuteronomy is called *V'zot Hab'rachah*. Each *parashah* has a corresponding haftarah. The haftarah is called by the same name as the *parashah*.

The following is a list of the names of all the פָּרָשִׁיּוֹת, the chapters and verses contained within each פָּרָשָׁה, and the corresponding haftarah portion.

	Torah Portion	**Haftarah Portion**[7]
Genesis		
B'reshit	1:1–6:8	Isaiah 42:5–43:10
Noach	6:9–11:32	Isaiah 54:1–55:5
Lech L'cha	12:1–17:27	Isaiah 40:27–41:16
Vayeira	18:1–22:24	2 Kings 4:1–37
Chayei	*Sarah*23:1–25:18	1 Kings 1:1–31
Tol'dot	25:19–28:9	Malachi 1:1–2:7
Vayetze	28:10–32:3	Hosea 12:13–14:10
Vayishlach	32:4–36:43	Hosea 1:7–12:12 or Obadiah 1:1–21[8]
Vayeshev	37:1–40:23	Amos 2:6–3:8
Miketz	41:1–44:17	1 Kings 3:15–4:1
Vayigash	44:18–47:27	Ezekiel 37:15–28
Vay'chi	47:28–50:26	1 Kings 2:1–12
Exodus		
Sh'mot	1:1–6:1	Isaiah 27:6–28:13; 29:22–23
Va-eira	6:2–9:35	Ezekiel 28:25–29:21
Bo	10:1–13:16	Jeremiah 46:13–38
B'shalach	13:17–17:16	Judges 4:4–5:31
Yitro	18:1–20:26	Isaiah 6:1–7:6, 9:5–6

---

[7] Sephardic readings frequently include different verses than those found on this list; for a full listing of all differences, please see *The Haftarah Commentary* by W. Gunther Plaut and Chaim Stern, pp. xi-xvi.

[8] Sephardim and some Ashkenazim read Obadiah.

	Torah Portion	**Haftarah Portion**
Mishpatim	21:1–24:18	Jeremiah 34:8–22; 33:25–26
T'rumah	25:1–27:19	1 Kings 5:26–6:13
T'tzaveh	27:20–30:10	Ezekiel 43:10–27
Ki Tisa	30:11–34:35	1 Kings 18:1–39
Vayakhel	35:1–38:20	1 Kings 7:40–50
P'kudei	38:21–40:38	1 Kings 7:51–8:21

Leviticus

Vayikra	1:1–5:26	Isaiah 43:21–44:23
Tzav	6:1–8:36	Jeremiah 7:21–8:3; 9:22–23
Sh'mini	9:1–11:47	2 Samuel 6:1–7:17
Tazri-a	12:1–13:59	2 Kings 4:42–5:19
M'tzora	14:1–15:33	2 Kings 7:3–20
Acharei Mot	16:1–18:30	Ezekiel 22:1–19
K'doshim	19:1–20:27	Amos 9:7–15
Emor	21:1–24:23	Ezekiel 44:15–31
B'har Sinai	25:1–26:2	Jeremiah 32:6–27
B'chukotai	26:3–27:34	Jeremiah 16:19–17:14

Numbers

B'midbar	1:1–4:20	Hosea 2:1–22
Naso	4:21–7:89	Judges 13:2–25
B'ha-alot'cha	8:1–12:16	Zechariah 2:14–4:7
Sh'lach-L'cha	13:1–15:41	Joshua 2:1–24
Korach	16:1–18:32	1 Samuel 11:14–12:22
Chukat	19:1–22:1	Judges 11:1–33
Balak	22:2–25:9	Micah 5:6–6:8
Pinchas	25:10–30:1	1 Kings 18:46–19:21
Matot	30:2–32:42	Jeremiah 1:1–2:3
Mas'ei	33:1–36:13	Jeremiah 2:4–28; 3:4

	Torah Portion	**Haftarah Portion**
Deuteronomy		
D'varim	1:1–3:22	Isaiah 1:1–27
Va-etchanan	3:23–7:11	Isaiah 40:1–26
Ekev	7:12–11:25	Isaiah 49:14–51:3
R'eh	11:26–16:17	Isaiah 54:11–55:5
Shof'tim	16:18–21:9	Isaiah 51:12–52:12
Ki Tetzei	21:10–25:19	Isaiah 54:1–10
Ki Tavo	26:1–29:8	Isaiah 60:1–22
Nitzavim	29:9–31:30	Isaiah 61:10–63:9
Vayelech	31:1–30	Isaiah 55:6–56:8
Ha-azinu	32:1–52	2 Samuel 22:1–51
V'zot Hab'rachah	33:1–34:12	Joshua 1:1–18

	Torah Portion	**Haftarah Portion**
Special *Shabbatot*		
Sh'kalim	Weekly *Parashah* + Exodus 30:11–16	2 Kings 12:1–17
Zachor (Shabbat before Purim)	Weekly *Parashah* + Deuteronomy 25:17–19	1 Samuel 15:2–34
Parah	Weekly *Parashah* + Numbers 19:1–22	Ezekiel 36:16–38
Hachodesh	Weekly *Parashah* + Exodus 12:1–20	Ezekiel 45:16–46:18
Hagadol (Shabbat before Pesach)	Weekly *Parashah*	Malachi 3:4–24
Shabbat Chazon (Shabbat before Tishah B'Av)	Weekly *Parashah*	Isaiah 1:1–27[9]
Rosh Chodesh (coinciding with Shabbat)	Weekly *Parashah* + Numbers 28:9–15	Isaiah 66:1–24
Machar Chodesh (day before Rosh Chodesh)	Weekly *Parashah*	1 Samuel 20:18–42

[9] The first and last verses are read with the usual haftarah tropes and the intervening ones with Lamentations trope. See Appendix G.

	Torah Portion	Haftarah Portion
High Holidays		
First Day Rosh Hashanah	(Traditional) Genesis 21:1–34 + Numbers 29:1–6 (Reform) Genesis 22:1–24	1 Samuel 1:1–2:10[10]
Second Day Rosh Hashanah	(Traditional) Genesis 22:1–24 + Numbers 29:1–6 (Reform) Genesis 1:1–2:3	Jeremiah 31:1–19
Shabbat Shuvah	Weekly *Parashah*	Hosea 14:2–10 + either Micah 7:18–20 *or* Joel 2:15–17[11]
Yom Kippur Morning	(Traditional) Leviticus 16:1–34 + Numbers 29:7–11 (Reform) Deuteronomy 29:9–14; 30:11–20	(Traditional) Isaiah 57:14–58:14 (Reform) Isaiah 58:1–14 only
Yom Kippur Afternoon	(Traditional) Leviticus 18:1–30 (Reform) Leviticus 19:1–4; 9–18; 32–37	(Traditional) Book of Jonah + Micah 7:18–20 (Reform) Book of Jonah

Festivals: Sukkot, Pesach, Shavuot

Sukkot First Day	Leviticus 22:26–23:24 (Traditional: + Numbers 29:12–16)	Zechariah 14:1–21
Sukkot Second Day	Same as above	1 Kings 8:2–21
Shabbat during Sukkot	Exodus 33:12–34:26 (Traditional: + Daily portion from Numbers.)	Ezekiel 38:18–39:16

---

[10] The Reform *machzor, Gates of Repentance*, offers a section from Nehemiah 8 as an alternative haftarah.

[11] When the weekly *sidra* is *Ha-azinu*, the corresponding haftarah is from Joel. When it is *Vayelech*, the haftarah is from Micah. Sephardim generally read Micah regardless of the *sidra*.

	Torah Portion	Haftarah Portion
Eighth Day (Sh'mini Atzeret)[12]	Deuteronomy 14:22–16:17 (Traditional: + Numbers 29:35–30:1)	1 Kings 8:54–66
Simchat Torah	Deuteronomy 33:1 to the end of Torah + Genesis 1:1–2:3 (Traditional: + Numbers 29:35–30:1)	Joshua 1:1–18
Pesach First Day	Exodus 12:21–51 (Traditional: + Numbers 28:16–25)	Joshua 3:5–7; 5:2–6:1, 27
Pesach Second Day	Leviticus 22:26–23:44 (Traditional: + Numbers 28:16–25)	2 Kings 23:1–9; 21–25
Shabbat during Pesach	Exodus 33:12–34:26	Ezekiel 36:37–37:14
Pesach Seventh Day	Exodus 13:17–15:26 (Traditional: + Numbers 28 :19–25)	2 Samuel 22:1–51
Pesach Eighth Day	Deuteronomy 15:19–16:17 (Traditional: + Numbers 28 :19–25)	Isaiah 10:32–12:6
Shavuot First Day	Exodus 19:1–20:23 (Traditional: + Numbers 28:26–31)	Ezekiel 1:1–28; 3:1
Shavuot Second Day	Deuteronomy 15:19–16:17[13] (Traditional: + Numbers 28:26–31)	Habakkuk 3:1–19

Other Days

Tishah B'Av Morning	Deuteronomy 4:25–40	Jeremiah 8:13–9:23
Tishah B'Av Afternoon	Exodus 32:11–14; 34:1–10	Isaiah 55:6–56:8[14]
Public Fasts	All readings as on the afternoon of Tishah B'Av	All readings as on the afternoon of Tishah B'Av[15]

---

[12] Most Reform congregations follow the Israeli calendar and celebrate Sh'mini Atzeret and Simchat Torah together. They usually read the Simchat Torah selections.

[13] If it falls on Shabbat: Deuteronomy 14:22–16:17.

[14] This is also the haftarah for *Vayelech;* Sephardim read from Hosea and Micah as on *Shabbat Shuvah.*

[15] Sephardim read no haftarah.

	Torah Portion	**Haftarah Portion**
Shabbat during Chanukah	Weekly *Parashah* (Traditional: + Numbers 7:1–11)	Zechariah 2:14–4:7
Second Shabbat Chanukah	Weekly *Parashah* (Traditional: Numbers 7:1–11)	1 Kings 7:40–50
Purim	Exodus 17:8–16	No haftarah
Yom HaShoah	Deuteronomy 4:30–40	Jeremiah 8:19–23
Yom Ha-Atzma-ut	Deuteronomy 11:8–21	Isaiah 10:32–12:6

In Tanach, chapter and verse numbers are often indicated with Hebrew letters rather than numbers. In this system, each letter of the Hebrew alphabet is assigned a numerical value.

For example, א = 1, ב = 2, י = 10, יג = 13, etc. Therefore, Isaiah 1:2 (chapter 1, verse 2) might be referred to as

יְשַׁעְיָהוּ א, ב

The only exceptions to this are the numbers 15 and 16. Following this logic, these would create a partial spelling of God's name (יה, יו). To avoid this, the conventional way of indicating 15 is by adding 9 + 6 (טו), and 16 is notated by adding 9 + 7 (טז).

On the right side of this page you will find a list of all letters and their numerical value.

א	1
ב ב	2
ג	3
ד	4
ה	5
ו	6
ז	7
ח	8
ט	9
י	10
ך כ כ	20
ל	30
ם מ	40
ן נ	50
ס	60
ע	70
ף פ פ	80
ץ צ	90
ק	100
ר	200
ש ש	300
ת	400

The blessing before the haftarah is chanted according to the haftarah cantillation and can be found on page 50 in this book, as well as on track 64 of the accompanying CD.

For the blessings after the haftarah, two versions follow below. First is the version found in most Reform prayer books; the traditional version is after that.

Blessing after the Haftarah (Reform)
as transcribed by Dr. Eliyahu Schleifer

Blessings after the Haftarah (Traditional)
as transcribed by Dr. Eliyahu Schleifer and A.W. Binder

4.*
SAM - CHEI - - - - NU A - DO - NAI E - LO - HEI - NU   B' - EI - LI - YA - HU HA - NA - VI   AV - DE - CHA

U - V'-MAL-CHUT BEIT DA-VID M'-SHI-CHE-CHA   BIM-HEI-RAH YA - VO_____   V'-YA - GEIL LI-BEI-NU.

AL KI-SO LO YEI-SHEV ZAR V'-LO YIN-CHA-LU OD A-CHEI-RIM ET K'-VO-DO_____   KI V'-SHEIM KOD-SH'-

CHA NISH - BA - TA LO   SHE-LO YICH - BEH   NEI - RO   L'-O-LAM VA - ED._____   BA -

RUCH A - TAH A - DO - NAI   MA - GEIN_____   DA - VID._____

5.
AL HA-TO-RAH_____   V'-AL HA-A-VO-DAH   V'-AL   HA-N'-VI-IM   V'-AL YOM HA-SHAB-BAT   HA-ZEH

SHE-NA-TA-TA LA - NU   A-DO-NAI   E-LO-HEI-NU   LI - K'-DU-SHAH

V'-LI - M'-NU-CHA_____   L'-CHA-VOD_____   U-L'-TIF-A-RET.   AL HA-KOL_____

A - DO - NAI   E - LO - HEI - NU   A - NACH-NU MO - DIM_____   LACH_____

U-M'-VA-R'-CHIM   O-TACH_____   YIT-BA-RACH   SHIM-CHA B'-FI KOL CHAI TA-MID L'-O-LAM

VA-ED._____   BA-RUCH A-TAH   A-DO-NAI M'-KA-DEISH HA-SHAB-BAT._____

21. מֻנַּח גֵּרְשַׁיִם
22. דַּרְגָּא
23. תְּבִיר
24. דַּרְגָּא תְּבִיר
25. מֵרְכָא תְּבִיר
26. קַדְמָא דַּרְגָּא תְּבִיר
27. קַדְמָא מֵרְכָא תְּבִיר
28. מֻנַּח דַּרְגָּא תְּבִיר
29. מֻנַּח תְּלִישָׁא גְדוֹלָה
30. מֻנַּח תְּלִישָׁא קְטַנָּה
31. מֻנַּח מֻנַּח פָּזֵר
32. זָקֵף גָּדוֹל
33. יְתִיב מֻנַּח קָטָן
34. יְתִיב קָטָן
35. מֻנַּח זַרְקָא מֻנַּח סְגוֹל
36. מֻנַּח זַרְקָא סְגוֹל
37. זַרְקָא מֻנַּח סְגוֹל
38. זַרְקָא סְגוֹל
39. מֵרְכָא כְּפוּלָה
40. מֵרְכָא טִפְחָא מֵרְכָא סוֹף־פָּסוּק:

(end of haftarah)

מְגִלָּה (_m'gillah_) is a general term that means "scroll." The scroll of Esther, _M'gillat Esther_, is frequently referred to as "The _M'gillah_," but in reality it is only one of five _M'gillot. M'gillat Esther_ is chanted on Purim, both during the evening and during the morning service. The trope functions in exactly the same way as the one you have learned, it has the exact same clauses, but the melodies of the _ta-amei hamikra_ are different. On pages 88–89 you will find the musical notation for Esther trope.

In Esther 7:9 you will find two tropes that are not found in any haftarah and that appear only once in the entire Torah: קַרְנֵי פָרָה and יָרֵחַ בֶּן יוֹמוֹ.

The first trope is the separator קַרְנֵי פָרָה (_karnei parah_), which looks exactly like a תְּלִישָׁא גְדוֹלָה and a תְּלִישָׁא קְטַנָּה stuck together:

This is how it sounds:

The second trope is יָרֵחַ בֶּן יוֹמוֹ (_yare-ach ben yomo_), which looks like an upside-down _etnachta_:

יָרֵחַ בֶּן יוֹמוֹ is the connector that appears before קַרְנֵי פָרָה.

Together they sound like this:

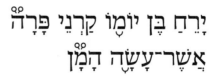

The Book of Esther has one very unusual distinction. Certain verses from Esther are not chanted to Esther trope at all, but rather to the cantillation of *Eicha* (Lamentations; see Appendix G). The cantillation for Esther, more than in any other book, specifically illustrates the text, often connecting it to a midrash. For example, *Midrash* Esther 2:11 tells us that the vessels used at Ahasuerus' feast were the same as those taken from the Temple by Nebuchadnezzar in 586 B.C. Therefore, the melody changes from the joyous trope of *M'gillat Esther* to the melodies of *Eicha*, the scroll traditionally read on Tishah B'Av.

The following verses in *M'gillat Esther* are chanted according to the trope for *Eicha*:
Esther 1:7, 2:6, 3:15, 4:1, 4:16.

In many communities, certain verses are sung to melodies rather than according to the trope, in ways that vary from one community to another. These verses might include: 1:22, 2:4, 2:15, 2:17, 4:14, 5:7, 5:13, 6:1, 6:10, 7:10, and 8:16. For examples, see *Biblical Chant* by A. W. Binder, or consult with your local expert.

In 9:7, the names of Haman's ten sons are chanted all on one note and in one breath, as quickly as possible.

The reading of *M'gillat Esther* is preceded and followed by blessings. Following are the notations for both blessings, based on transcriptions by A. W. Binder and Dr. Eliyahu Schleifer.

Blessings before the Reading of *M'gillat Esther*

1.

BA - RUCH_____ A - TAH_____ A - DO - NAI E - LO - HEI - NU ME - LECH HA - O - LAM A - SHER

KI - D' - SHA - NU B' - MITZ - VO - TAV_____ V' - TZI - VA - NU AL MI - KRAH M' - GI - LAH._____

2.

BA - RUCH_____ A - TAH_____ A - DO - NAI E - LO - HEI - NU ME - LECH HA - O - LAM_____

SHE - A - SAH NI - SIM LA - A - VO - TEI - NU BA - YA - MIM HA - HEIM BA - Z'MAN HA - ZEH._____

3.

BA - RUCH_____ A - TAH_____ A - DO - NAI E - LO - HEI - NU ME - LECH

HA - O - LAM_____ SHE - HE - CHE - YA - NU V' - KI - YI - MA - NU V' - HI - GI - YA - NU LAZ -

MAN HA - ZEH._____

83 ## Blessing after the Reading of *M'gillat Esther*

(The text in brackets may be omitted in Reform synagogues.)

(end of each chapter)

Cantillation for *Shir HaShirim* (Song of Songs), Ruth, and *Kohelet* (Ecclesiastes)

The Scrolls, or *M'gillot*, of *Shir HaShirim* (Song of Songs), Ruth, and *Kohelet* (Ecclesiastes) all use the same trope melodies and are chanted on the Three Festivals.

Shir HaShirim is traditionally read on the intermediate Shabbat during the week of Passover or on the first day of Passover if it falls on the Sabbath.

Ruth is read on the second day of Shavuot (in many Reform congregations, where Shavuot is observed for one day, the book of Ruth is read on that day.)

Kohelet is read on the intermediate Shabbat of Sukkot or on the last day of the festival.

Below you will find the musical notation for the tropes.

32. זָקֵף גָּדוֹל

33. יְתִיב מֻנַּח קָטֹן

34. יְתִיב קָטֹן

35. מֻנַּח זַרְקָא מֻנַּח סֶגוֹל

36. מֻנַּח זַרְקָא סֶגוֹל

37. זַרְקָא מֻנַּח סֶגוֹל

38. זַרְקָא סֶגוֹל

39. מֵרְכָא טִפְחָא מֵרְכָא סוֹף־פָּסוּק:
(end of each chapter)

39a. מֵרְכָא טִפְחָא מֵרְכָא סוֹף־פָּסוּק:
(end of book)

The scroll of *Eicha* is read on the evening of Tishah B'Av. This scroll is read with a sense of mourning and chanted at a slow tempo because it describes the grief and desolation brought on by the destruction of the Temple in Jerusalem, and the subsequent slaughter and exile of the Jews by the Babylonians in 586 B.C.E.

On the Shabbat before Tishah B'Av, *Shabbat Chazon, Eicha* cantillation is introduced in the haftarah reading in the following manner: The first and last verses are chanted according to the trope for *Eicha,* and the intermediate verses according to the regular haftarah trope.

On the morning of Tishah B'Av, the haftarah is read according to *Eicha* cantillation, except for the last two verses, which are chanted according to the regular haftarah trope.

Eicha trope is also used for certain verses of Esther (see Appendix E, page 85).

Below you will find the musical notation for the tropes.

86

.10 מִדְהַפָּ֤ךְ פַּשְׁטָא֙ מֻ֣נַח קָטֹ֔ן

.11 מִדְהַפָּ֤ךְ פַּשְׁטָא֙ קָטֹ֔ן

.12 פַּשְׁטָא֙ מֻ֣נַח קָטֹ֔ן

.13 פַּשְׁטָא֙ קָטֹ֔ן

.14 מֻ֣נַח מַהְפָּ֤ךְ פַּשְׁטָא֙ מֻ֣נַח קָטֹ֔ן

.15 קַדְמָ֨א וְאַזְלָ֜א

.16 גֵּ֜רֶשׁ

.17 מֻנַּ֣ח׀ מֻ֣נַח רְבִיעִ֗י

.18 מֻ֣נַח רְבִיעִ֗י

.19 רְבִיעִ֗י

.20 גֵּרְשַׁ֞יִם

.21 מֻ֣נַח גֵּרְשַׁ֞יִם

.22 דַּרְגָּ֧א

.23 תְּבִ֛יר

.24 דַּרְגָּ֧א תְּבִ֛יר

.25 מֵרְכָ֧א תְּבִ֛יר

.26 קַדְמָ֨א דַּרְגָּ֧א תְּבִ֛יר

.27 קַדְמָ֨א מֵרְכָ֧א תְּבִ֛יר

.28 מֻ֣נַח דַּרְגָּ֧א תְּבִ֛יר

.29 מֻ֣נַח תְּלִישָׁ֥א גְדוֹלָ֖ה

30. מֻנַּח   תְּלִישָׁא קְטַנָּהֿ

31. זָקֵף גָּדֿוֹל

32. יְתִיב   מֻנַּח   קָטֹן

33. יְתִיב   קָטֹן

34. מֻנַּח   זַרְקָא   מֻנַּח   סְגֿוֹל

35. מֻנַּח   זַרְקָא   סְגֿוֹל

36. זַרְקָא   מֻנַּח   סְגֿוֹל

37. זַרְקָא   סְגֿוֹל

38. מֵרְכָא טִפְחָא מֵרְכָא סוֹף־פָּסֽוּק:
(end of each chapter)

Aliyah (plural, *aliyot*) עֲלִיָּה / עֲלִיּוֹת: Literally, "ascent." The honor extended to a congregant whereby she or he is called up to the reading of the Torah. The following is the traditional number of *aliyot* for reading the Torah:

- Weekdays (Monday and Thursday): Three *aliyot*
- Rosh Chodesh (New Month): Four on a weekday; seven plus *maftir* on Shabbat
- Fast Days: Three at morning service; three at afternoon service (the third is *maftir*)
- Rosh Hashanah: Five plus *maftir* on a weekday; seven plus *maftir* on Shabbat
- Yom Kippur: Six plus *maftir* on a weekday; seven plus *maftir* on Shabbath; three (the third is *maftir*) at afternoon service
- Three Festivals (Pesach, Shavuot, Sukkot): Five plus *maftir* on a weekday; seven plus *maftir* on Shabbat; four on *Chol Hamoeid*
- Shabbat: Seven plus *maftir*

Amen אָמֵן: Literally, "So be it." The response recited after hearing a blessing.

Aron Hakodesh אֲרוֹן הַקֹּדֶשׁ: The Holy Ark, which is used to house the Torah scrolls.

Atzei Chayim (singular, *etz chayim*) עֲצֵי / עֵץ חַיִּים: Literally, "trees of life." The wooden handles of the Torah.

Aufruf: From the Yiddish "to call up." Calling up of the bride and groom to the Torah for an *aliyah* on the Shabbat before their wedding.

Avnet אַבְנֵט: The belt that holds the Torah scroll, which is closed when the Torah is not in use.

Ba-al/Ba-alat Koreh/K'riyah בַּעַל / בַּעֲלַת קוֹרֵא / קְרִיאָה: The individual who reads aloud from the Torah for the congregation.

Bimah בִּימָה: The pulpit or reader's desk.

Birkat Hagomel בִּרְכַּת הַגּוֹמֵל: A special benediction recited during the Torah service by anyone who has escaped a serious danger, such as illness, accident, etc.

Chazak, chazak, v'nitchazek חֲזַק חֲזַק וְנִתְחַזֵּק: "From strength to strength, let us strengthen one another." At the end of each *sefer* in the Torah are blank lines. When the reader reaches that point, she or he should stop and allow the congregation to chant the words *Chazak, chazak, v'nitchazek*. Then the reader repeats, *Chazak, chazak, v'nitchazek*.

Chumash חוּמָשׁ: Literally, "fifth." The first five books of the Bible, referred to as the Five Books of Moses. Pentateuch is the Greek term for *Chumash*.

Dikduk דִקְדוּק: Grammar.

Gabai גַּבַּאי: The synagogue functionary who assists during the public reading of Torah.

G'lilah גְּלִילָה: The tying/dressing of the Torah scroll.

Goleil (m.)/*Golelet* (f.) גּוֹלֵל / גּוֹלֶלֶת: The person who ties the Torah scroll and dresses it after the reading.

Haftarah הַפְטָרָה: The reading from Prophets that follows Shabbat and holiday Torah readings.

Hagbahah הַגְבָּהָה: The raising of the Torah at the conclusion of the reading.

Hakafah (plural, *hakafot*) הַקָּפָה / הַקָּפוֹת: The processional through the synagogue with the Torah scroll before and/or after the Torah reading.

Keter Torah כֶּתֶר תּוֹרָה: The crownlike ornament that is placed atop the Torah scroll (different from *rimonim*).

K'riyat HaTorah קְרִיאַת הַתּוֹרָה: The public reading of Torah in the synagogue.

K'ri uch'tiv קְרִי וּכְתִיב: Literally, "read and written." An instance in which the way a word is actually read from the Torah is different from the written text.

Mafsik (plural, *mafsikim*) מַפְסִיק / מַפְסִיקִים: The general name for a cantillation mark that functions as a separator.

Maftir מַפְטִיר: Both the last *aliyah* and the last person to be called up to the reading of Torah. Often that person also reads the haftarah.

Magbiah(m.)/*Magbihah*(f.) מַגְבִּיהַּ / מַגְבִּיהָהּ: The person who is called up to raise the Torah scroll in front of the congregation at the conclusion of the reading.

M'chaber (plural, *m'chabrim*) מְחַבֵּר / מְחַבְּרִים: The general name for a cantillation mark that functions as a connector.

Meteg מֶתֶג: Accent mark used to indicate secondary accents in Torah.

M'il מְעִיל: The Torah mantle.

Minhag מִנְהָג: Custom.

Minhag Hamakom מִנְהַג הַמָּקוֹם: Literally, "custom of the place." The term for following the custom of the community in which a person is praying.

Ner Tamid נֵר תָּמִיד: The Eternal Light.

Parashah (plural, *parashiyot* or *parashot*) פָּרָשָׁה / פָּרָשִׁיּוֹת / פָּרָשׁוֹת: A section or part. The specific section of Torah assigned for reading in the synagogue each week and on each festival, fast, and Holy Day.

Parashat Hashavu-a פָּרָשַׁת הַשָּׁבוּעַ: The Torah portion of the week.

Pasuk פָּסוּק: A verse or sentence.

Pasul פָּסוּל: Ritually unfit.

Pentateuch: See *Chumash*.

Perek (plural, *p'rakim*) פֶּרֶק / פְּרָקִים: Chapter.

P'sik פְּסִיק: A vertical line between two words indicating a short pause. Exception: When a *p'sik* is found between two *munachim* and is then followed by a *r'vi-i*, the *p'sik* is a part of *munach l'garmeih*.

P'tuchah פְּתוּחָה: Literally, "opening." The open space at the end of a *pasuk* in the *Sefer Torah*, indicated in the *Chumash* by the letter פ.

Rimonim (singular, *rimon*) רִימוֹנִים / רִימוֹן: "Pomegranates." Ornaments that adorn each wooden pole of the wrapped Torah scroll.

Sefer (plural, *s'farim*) סֵפֶר / סְפָרִים: Book.

Sefer Torah (plural, *Sifrei Torah*) סֵפֶר / סִפְרֵי תּוֹרָה: The actual Torah scroll used during worship, as opposed to a printed *Chumash*.

Sidrah סִדְרָה: The weekly portion of the Torah, used interchangeably with *parashah*.

S'tumah סְתוּמָה (also *s'gurah*): Literally, "closed." The closed space at the end of a *pasuk* in the *Sefer Torah*, indicated by the letter ס.

Ta-am (plural, *t'amim*) טַעַם / טְעָמִים: Literally, "taste" or "sense"; also "accent." A cantillation mark or symbol.

Ta-amei Hamikra טַעֲמֵי הַמִּקְרָא: Cantillation symbols.

Tanach תנ"ך: The term *Tanach* is derived from the first letters of the names of its three sections: **T**orah (the Five Books of Moses), **N**'vi-im (Prophets), and **K(Ch)**'tuvim (Writings; e.g., Psalms, Proverbs, the five *M'gillot*).

Trope: Cantillation, from the Greek word tropos (τροποσ), meaning "style" or "way."

Yad יָד: Literally, "hand." The pointer used by a Torah reader.

Avenary, Hanoch. *The Ashkenazic Tradition of Biblical Chant Between 1500 and 1900.* Tel Aviv: Tel Aviv University Press, 1978.

Binder, A. W. *Biblical Chant.* New York: Philosophical Library, 1959.

Contzius, Erik L. F. *Chant That Trope.* Elkins Park, Pa.: Self-published, 1999.

Encyclopedia Judaica. "Cantillation," "Masoretic Accents," "Masorah." Jerusalem: Keter Publishing House, 1972.

Idelsohn, A. Z. *Jewish Music in Its Historical Development.* Westport, Conn.: Greenwood Press, 1981.

Jacobson, Joshua. *Chanting the Hebrew Bible: The Sense of Cantillation.* Philadelphia: Jewish Publication Society, forthcoming.

Kadari, Y'hudah. *V'shinantam L'vanecha.* Jerusalem: R'nanot, Hamachon L'muzikah Y'hudit, 1994.

Leneman, Helen. *Bar/Bat Mitzvah Education.* Denver: A.R.E. Publishing, 1993.

Rosenbaum, Samuel. *A Guide to Haftarah Chanting.* Hoboken, N.J.: Ktav Publishing House, 1973.

Rosenberg, Yitzchok Mordechai. *T'aamim L'korim.* New York: Chadish Press, 1980.

Rosowsky, Solomon. *Cantillation of the Bible.* New York: Reconstructionist Press, 1957.

Schleifer, Eliyahu. "Cantillation" in *Encyclopedia of Judaism.* Jerusalem: 1989.

Shiloah, Amnon. *Jewish Musical Traditions.* Detroit: Wayne State University Press, 1992.

Simon, Ely. *The Complete Torah Reading Handbook.* Brooklyn: The Judaica Press, 1996.

Spiro, Pinchas. *Haftarah Chanting.* New York: Board of Jewish Education, 1978.

_____. *Teachers' Guide to Haftarah Chanting.* New York: Cantors Assembly, 1995.

Werner, Eric. *A Voice Still Heard.* University Park: Pennsylvania State University Press, 1976.

Notes

Notes

Notes

Notes

Notes

Notes

Notes

Notes

Notes

Notes

Notes

Notes